Open Government

Also in the same series:

Seeing Ourselves
 – interpreting contemporary society

Libby Purves, Robert Blake, Dahah Zohar &
John Habgood

The Retreat of the State
 – nurturing the soul of society

Nigel Lawson, Arthur Seldon, Michael Taylor &
David Owen

Ink and Spirit
 – literature and spirituality

Ronald Blythe, Penelope Lively, Richard Marsh,
David Scott & A.N. Wilson

Open Government

What should we really know?

Kate Adie, Peter Hennessy,
Gerard J. Hughes SJ,
Douglas Hurd and
John Major

Edited and introduced by
Stephen Platten

CANTERBURY
PRESS
Norwich

First published in 2003 by the Canterbury Press Norwich
(a publishing imprint of Hymns Ancient &
Modern Limited, a registered charity)
St Mary's Works, St Mary's Plain
Norwich, Norfolk, NR3 3BH

British Library Cataloguing in Publication data

A catalogue record for this book is available
from the British Library

ISBN 1-85311-482-0

Typeset by Regent Typesetting, London
and printed in Great Britain by
Biddles Ltd, www.biddles.co.uk

Contents

About the Contributors

Kate Adie is Chief News Correspondent with the BBC.

Peter Hennessy is a former lobby correspondent with *The Times* and is now Attlee Professor of Contemporary British History at Queen Mary College, University of London.

Gerard J. Hughes SJ is Master of Campion Hall, Cambridge, and a moral philosopher and theologian.

The Rt Hon. Lord Hurd of Westwell is High Steward of Westminster Abbey and a former Home Secretary and Foreign Secretary.

John Major was Prime Minister from 1990–1997.

Stephen Platten is Dean of Norwich and teaches theology.

Introduction

STEPHEN PLATTEN

. . . we are the impostors who speak the truth, the unknown men whom all men know . . . we have spoken very frankly to you, we have opened our hearts wide to you all . . . open wide your hearts to us.

II Corinthians 6: 8, 11, 13

Truth and Secrecy

'Thieves broke into the Kremlin yesterday and stole next year's Soviet general election results; a spokesman said that the leak was regrettable and that steps were being taken to ensure future security of information for the good of the people.' Such humour was commonplace in commentary on current affairs before the collapse of Communism in the Soviet Union and Eastern Europe. Dictatorships and totalitarian regimes breed a culture of secrecy and misinformation. Power in both Hitler's Germany and Stalin's USSR rested to a large degree on the control of information centrally by the state; the KGB was a key office of the state within the Soviet system and it is no surprise that attitudes cultivated within such a climate persist, even in an avowedly democratic Russia. A senior British diplomat commenting on the fall of Ceauşescu's Romania said that the entire society had depended upon a complex network of informers and upon a culture of lies: 'It would take at least a generation before people could once again learn to appreciate the essence of a society based upon truth.'

Totalitarian societies come to depend upon secrecy and deceit. So the mystery which surrounded the long and lingering death of President Tito of Yugoslavia was mirrored time and again as the Soviet Union staggered towards collapse, with the illness and death of first Brezhnev, then Andropov and finally Chernenko. As in life so in death; secrecy and never openness remained the order of the day. At the heart of this nexus of issues lie questions of truth and openness within government and more widely within civil society. The answers are of major concern to democratic societies supposedly built upon an open relationship between governors and governed. Democratic politicians may espouse in their manifestoes the principle of open government, but it can easily become nothing but a slogan, as Peter Hennessy makes clear towards the end of his reflections in this book. Quoting Robert Hazell, he notes: 'Open government means the Government publishing information largely for its own purposes: information that the Government thinks we need to know or might like to know. Freedom of information requires the Government to disclose information which we decide for ourselves we want to know.'[1]

Introduction

Central to this debate, then, are issues of transparency in government dealings and notably with the media in contemporary society. The word transparency is 'in the air' even as this introduction is being written. As Britain awaited the inauguration of a new law requiring political parties to disclose the names of those giving large donations to their cause, so the government momentarily closed ranks before revealing the late Lord Hamlyn as the donor of £2 million to Labour Party funds. Secrecy within government can become almost a 'knee jerk' reaction. This book brings together a set of reflections focusing on open government, freedom of information and transparency of response within public life. It does so also within the context of a Cathedral Institute, an institution dedicated to reflecting upon theology in the context of public life. Indeed this was the first set of Launcelot Fleming Lectures to be sponsored by the University of East Anglia and Norwich Cathedral through the auspices of Norwich Cathedral Institute which they jointly sponsor along with the Diocese of Norwich.

Open Theology?

Nevertheless, despite this context it can by no means be assumed that the Christian Church or Christian theology has been universally supportive of the principles of freedom, transparency and openness. At the beginning of his chapter, Gerard Hughes makes this point with some irony:

Stephen Platten

I would not suppose that the Roman Catholic Church, whatever her many virtues, can be held up as a distinguished example of open government. Perhaps worst of all, I am a Jesuit – and are we Jesuits not notorious for the practice of secrecy, and the theory of equivocation and mental reservation when forced to account for ourselves in tricky situations?[2]

All of these issues were brought together within a thriller published just as the Soviet Union was imploding through the corruption of its own institutions.[3] The thriller tells of the appointment and of the exploits of two new private secretaries, one elected to serve a thinly-veiled Mikhail Gorbachev and the other to serve a thinly-veiled Pope John Paul II. The research behind the book is exceptional and issues of openness and secrecy weave in and out of the text alongside other political issues. At one point the narrator notes:

The apostolic nuncio in Washington had made it very clear that Zingler's draft for the Pope's letter to the American bishops' conference was disastrous. The United States was a nation founded on democratic ideals: the right to freedom of speech, the right to question traditional teaching, the right to express a view on social issues, all these were held to be the birthright of every American citizen. It had taken the Church nearly two hundred years to establish itself as genuinely American and not some foreign import . . . The Church in Rome simply could not sack theologians

from Catholic-funded posts at American universities
for merely asking questions . . .[4]

In theory the Roman Catholic Church, along with other
mainstream churches, is committed to the very opposite
of such secrecy and autocracy. Christianity is committed
to nurturing our full humanity within an open community. In an excellent document on social ethics addressed
to British voters before the 1997 General Election, the
Roman Catholic Bishops' Conference for England and
Wales noted: 'It is in [this] spirit of openness, and of
listening as well as teaching, that the Catholic Bishops'
Conference of England and Wales looks ahead to the
General Election that is expected in the coming
months.'[5] This implies an openness and transparency
within the Church of God as well as within wider society.

Theology and Open Government

As Gerard Hughes indicates, it is difficult, if not impossible, to bring any direct Christian teaching to the issue of
open government. Neither the Bible nor tradition has
focused upon this question. Even so, freedom of information, transparency and open government are all issues
which provoke questions on the manner in which the
Church conducts its own affairs and on the theological
doctrines and principles upon which it believes its own
polity to be based. It is certainly the case that philosophical and theological assumptions can affect the manner
in which a society or an institution within society

conducts or governs itself. These issues were debated plainly half a century ago in Karl Popper's magisterial two-volume discussion *The Open Society and Its Enemies.*[6] Plato, with his intellectual elite and his fierce censorship, was seen to be the classical culprit. The chief culprit of modern Europe was deemed by Popper to be G. W. H. Hegel with his idealized philosophical framework which itself formed the matrix upon which Karl Marx, Popper's second modern culprit, could base his dialectical materialism. Popper was suspicious of such thoroughgoing deterministic ideologies and opted instead for a more pragmatic pattern of reflective social engineering. Christian theology has also had a crucial responsibility for helping form patterns of government, civilization and polity at least since the Constantinian settlement. These patterns have not always been creditable. Where precisely have theology and practice taken the Judaeo-Christian tradition, then, over at least the past three millennia?

With regard to the Old Testament the answer is complex, if for no other reason than for the unfolding historical scenario spread out over a period of at least one thousand years. Before the fall of first the northern kingdom of Israel, and then the southern kingdom of Judaea, there certainly developed a policy which bound together religion and the state. The wealth of differing historical interpretations of development in ancient Israel generally agree on the fact that religion was used to strengthen Israel's national self-consciousness and that it was used to support these small kingdoms as they strug-

gled with their predator neighbours; the king was himself seen as the vice-gerent of God, a divine ambassador
who helped focus religious and political loyalties. The
growth of the so-called Deuteronomic theology saw this
in terms of a specific pattern of *salvation history*, rooted
in the worship of the one true God of Israel, Yahweh.
The book of Deuteronomy itself and the writings of the
Deuteronomic historian in I and II Samuel, and I and II
Kings, all aim at focusing loyalty on the one shrine at
Zion, that is within the royal and holy city of Jerusalem.
It has to be said that little of this literature bears witness
to principles of 'open government', although it does
certainly see religion and politics as being closely inter-
twined.

By the time of Jesus this process had seen its vicissi-
tudes, first with the collapse of both kingdoms, then a
period of exile in Babylon and eventually the emergence
of a form of protectorate status under the Persian king,
Cyrus. Later still, after the Seleucid conquest of Israel
came the triumph of Rome during which period there
was effectively theocratic self-government by the high-
priestly family in Jerusalem. (This was the situation into
which Jesus of Nazareth was born.) All this further
suggests an intricate involvement of religion with politics
within Israel. This, then, was the Jewish background to
the rise of Christianity. It is difficult to assess how the
embryonic Christian community related to the state;
things probably varied from place to place. It would be
premature to talk of a Church in New Testament times,
but already different stances towards the civil authorities

are encountered in the different writings brought together there. Amongst the evangelists it is Luke who is
perhaps keenest to adjust to the reality of the Roman
state; the story he tells is one where Christianity is not to
be seen as a threat to the imperial overlords. Paul too, in
the famous passage in Romans 13 is keen to suggest that
the embryonic Christian community is not there to react
to the state. Instead he implies that God's grace stands
behind those who have been granted civil power, 'There
is no authority but by act of God, and the existing
authorities are instituted by him' (Romans 13: 1).

Openness in the Christian Community

Perhaps more interesting with regard to our main theme,
however, is Paul's teaching about the nature of the
Christian community itself. Here his imagery of the *body*
and the working together of its many numbers suggest
an organic model. This is spelt out in most detail in I
Corinthians 12 and it reaches a climax when he argues in
v. 26, 'If one organ suffers, they all suffer together. If one
flourishes, they all rejoice together.' This Pauline doctrine
of the body implies an openness and dependence of each
part of the body to every other part and to the whole. In
different ways this Pauline doctrine of the body has
formed the foundation for theologies of the Church in
ensuing centuries. Perhaps two key lessons follow. The
first is about the corporate nature of the Christian faith.
Although an *individual's* faith and an *individual's*
relationship with Christ is essential, so is that individual

also ineluctably caught up into the whole. The community as a whole is in relationship with God through Christ; there is effectively a 'political' implication here – the Christian faith is lived out within community and not in individual isolation.

The second lesson relates to openness within the body. Interdependence requires mutual respect and transparency if the community is to prosper. At its best these two lessons may have 'missionary' implications within wider society. The Christian model of human flourishing is within an open, interdependent and transparent community

As Gerard Hughes hints at the beginning of his analysis, this has by no means been the consistent and continuing experience of the Christian community throughout the ages. Stumbling blocks have been encountered in a variety of different patterns of Christian polity. Calvin's theocratic experiment in sixteenth-century Geneva met an early and untimely end. Cromwell's Puritan Commonwealth was not the model of a redeemed community. The Papacy with its involvement in temporal power tells its own story. Pius IX and the Syllabus of Errors are but one low watermark in the efforts of the Christian Church to live out its life as an organic functioning body of Christ, transparent to the world. But it is not only within the body itself that the Church has failed to be an exemplary model of Christian life. At different moments in its history the Church has offered anything but openness towards wider society; the martyrdom of Giordano Bruno for his assumed heresy, and the trial of Galileo

Galilei are particular glaring failures. And Roman Catholicism is by no means uniquely guilty. The history of the fate of Darwin's theories and its exponents at the hands of Bishop Wilberforce and the Church of England has been much embroidered, but the kernel of the story is still a failure of openness and freedom of thought. Orthodoxy too, during the twentieth-century dominance of Eastern Europe by Communism has had a far from unblemished record in this regard.

Christianity and Society

It is, of course, all too easy to catalogue failings both within the Church's own body and in its dealings with the wider world. What signals might the Christian community be offering to contemporary society and what dangers does it face itself, in the light of current trends within society? Starting with incipient dangers, perhaps the danger which is most acute is that of *privatization*. It is a tendency which assails not only religion but so much of our contemporary experience. There is an irony in the fact that in a world which is being transformed by the effects of *globalization*, our lives are increasingly threatened by privatization and isolation. The reasons for these trends are many and complex. Earlier agrarian and industrial societies were generally community-based. Within the countryside, villages and market towns depended upon organic communities; agricultural workers, farmers and local traders worked together within comparatively small interdependent social units. The advent of the industrial revolution, which undoubtedly introduced repetitive and soul-destroying automation alongside work which was often both anti-social in its hours and physically demanding, nevertheless begat new communities. Mining towns, steel works, and also the 'back-to-backs' of the East End of London all breathed their own sense of interdependence and community. The growth of a broader middle class and the demographic changes caused by further automation and the information revolution have reduced that sense of community; the nuclear family has largely replaced the extended family.

In the second half of the twentieth century there was also an intellectual shift towards the primacy of the individual. Existentialist philosophy combined with insights from psychoanalytic theory together enhanced the cult of the individual. Indeed at one point 'doing one's own thing' became the motto of the age. It is now commonplace to note the demise of institutions and associations. It is not only the churches who have lost members; political parties, uniformed organizations and every other form of association now find it more difficult to persuade people to commit themselves. Finally, the computer revolution unavoidably increases this sense of privatization. Computers by their very nature engage the individual. In our contemporary world, sophisticated roles can now be fulfilled from the comfort of a person's own home; the gismo passes the assembled material down through the electronic ether without any need to bring people together in offices. Some even see education as going in that same direction; in this scenario colleges and schools would become institutions of a past age as people respond to programmes of learning, sitting at their computer terminals back at home. Without indulging in fanciful *futurology* the point is clear. Our lives have become increasingly privatized. So much of human activity is now related more and more exclusively to the private sphere of life.

This tendency can itself undermine all those instincts which would build towards a more open and relational society. The significance of the media in this process is underlined by both Kate Adie and Douglas Hurd in their contributions to this collection. As they both suggest, it is easy to blame the media for their role in interpreting and influencing developments within society. But this is a two-way phenomenon. Douglas Hurd's title, 'The Media We Deserve', captures this precisely. Newspapers, radio and television will tend to produce and place on offer that which the consumer desires. We cannot blame populism in the press if we are still prepared to buy those same newspapers, in order to read those sensationalist stories which in another mood we would condemn. Privatization allows us to buy into that which is on offer rather than to engage ourselves with the political process. In the past four years there has been much comment about the decreasing significance of the role of Parliament; we are manipulated, we believe, by Downing Street press secretaries and the 'spin-doctors' of the political machine. But Alistair Campbell is not the first of a new cadre. After all both Bernard Ingham and Charles Powell were castigated for the way in which they mediated the policies of both the Thatcher and Major governments to the British public.

A Responsive Society?

These reflections suggest that the road towards freedom of information, open government and transparency in public life is a far more interactive process than is often assumed or claimed. The openness for which Peter Hennessy so engagingly and eagerly argues will not be achieved if we collude with a media and PR-led world operating on the consumer-directed model which is so essential to market economies. Even the market requires monitoring and some control, if the might of the rich and powerful is not to crush the helplessness of the weak and more vulnerable. In other words, open government and freedom of information assume a responsive society.

This may be the point to return to the religious context and the contribution which might be offered from the Christian tradition. Religion has not been immune to the pressures of privatization. Indeed some might argue that religion, or the Christian tradition, has been privatization's most significant victim. The tendency towards privatization within religion has again come about through two rather different sets of pressures both from within and outside the Church. From within, as Christianity has been further marginalized, so churches have tended increasingly to concentrate on their own internal structures and theological preoccupations. In certain spheres within the Christian community, this is also accompanied by a greater emphasis on the personal faith of the individual; this personal strand becomes divorced from the implications of faith for life in society as a whole; the corporate responsibility of the Church is allowed to shrink. This shift has been reinforced by some contemporary theological trends which argue that it is both arrogant and unrealistic for the Church to engage with society and politics directly; such engagement, they argue, compromises the gospel. John Habgood summarizes these approaches well: 'The emphasis is rather on the prophetic import of a transcendent faith. There are frequent references to the corrupting effect of trying to be socially significant. Better a privatized gospel in its purity than a publicly acceptable religion which has lost its soul.'[7]

From outside the Christian community, political tendencies can often support such a shift. The engagement of the Church of England with urban issues in the 1980s, and notably in *Faith in the City*, was often condemned by politicians as an example of the Church interfering in politics.

Earlier analysis in this introduction, however, suggests a very different background and context from the history of the Judaeo-Christian tradition. Even when the engagement has been wrong-headed and misinformed there has been a continued commitment to an interweaving of theology and society. The roots are there in the Old Testament and certainly they reappear as a subject for debate in the New Testament writings. From the heroic witness of the early Church into the Constantinian era when the empire embraced the Christian gospel, engagement between Church and society has been continuous in one manner or another. Also at the heart of this has lain a theology of the Church which could not ignore Paul's injunctions about the *body of Christ*. The key role played by the Benedictine tradition and the rise of the monasteries in the growth of European culture equally should not be forgotten. Even the consultative model of the role of the Abbot described in the *Rule of St Benedict* has played its part in the development of western democracy. Neither Church nor state has (or indeed can) take over this model directly since it could imply a paternalism which would be unacceptable. Nevertheless the main intention of the model is sound; the Abbot's responsibility was to consult continuously and openly with the entire community. His discernment on behalf of the community would then be one which focused a consensus that could only issue from an open and transparent process of consultation.

This, then, may be the key contribution which the Christian tradition can still offer to society as a whole. The Church will do so with a realistic humility offering insights which might strengthen a tendency and commitment to openness of government and freedom of information for the betterment of the common good. All this assumes that the churches and theologians will not collude with the forces of privatization but rather challenge them prophetically. Instead of becoming the chief captive of this tendency, the Christian Church has the responsibility of re-affirming the significance of inter-dependence within local, national and international communities. This assumes a rediscovery of an organic model within the Christian Church itself and then an engagement of that community with society both nation-ally and internationally. Two prophets, one from either side of the Atlantic, suggest themselves as twentieth-century models of this approach.

During some of the darkest days of Europe, in the course of the Second World War, it was Bishop George Bell of Chichester who with Dietrich Bonhoeffer offered a prophetic challenge to the leaders of the nations on both sides of the conflict. Their revulsion at the tyranny of Hitler could never be doubted, but they called for an open response by governments to calls for humanitarian considerations on both the policy of obliteration bombing and on efforts directed towards a negotiated settlement. Bell was not popular for his stance either in the Church or in the wider political sphere. Some have suggested that he forfeited further preferment on account of his outspoken interventions. If that is so it does not speak well of the openness of the political process.

Across the Atlantic, both the work and the intellectual engagement of Reinhold Niebuhr is perhaps the para-mount example. Niebuhr was a realist who believed that the context of the Christian gospel offered the most effective analysis of the human condition not only indi-vidually but corporately too; the title of one of his most penetrating books captures this precisely: *Moral Man and Immoral Society*.[8] Niebuhr believed that only a realistic acceptance of the fallenness of human nature could open up the political process to the realities of the corruption of power within and between nations. That realism might underpin an effective acceptance of both the need for and the means of achieving both openness in government and transparency in the conduct of public life.

Following on from Niebuhr's analysis of human nature and the need for a healthy Christian realism, a further point arises in relation to openness in government. One of the effects of such openness is ineluctably to disperse power. Much of the instinct behind secrecy is that knowledge is power and this means control. Open government allows for a greater sharing of power through dispersion and decentralization. Often people despair both within and outside the churches at the plethora of synods, episcopal conferences and councils. Nevertheless, within reason, this variety of checks and balances allows for an effective dispersion of power which is a model for polity within society and within government. A quotation from Niebuhr may be both a salutary ending for this introduction and also an appropriate theological launch pad for the essays which follow:

Nothing worth doing is completed in our lifetime; therefore we must be saved by hope. Nothing true or beautiful or good makes complete sense in any immediate context of history; therefore we must be saved by faith. Nothing we do, however virtuous, can be accomplished alone; therefore we are saved by love.

No virtuous act is quite as virtuous from the stand-point of our friend or foe as from our own standpoint. Therefore we must be saved by the final form of love, which is forgiveness.[9]

No – I Haven't Got News For You

KATE ADIE

Learning the Hard Way

As the most junior member of staff on a local radio station in north-east England many years ago, I was privileged to get the jobs that no one else would do. I read the fat stock reports, not understanding a word of them, fed the station cat – our main defence against our studio cables being chewed by ravenous Geordie mice – and invented weather forecasts for the early morning show. As an extra privilege, I produced the weekly religious programme, which involved fending off rapacious evangelical sects who saw our transmitter as a beacon dedicated to their message, and explaining to charming vicars that the *Thought for the Day* spot did not accommodate half-hour monologues.

Nowhere in all of these duties did the notion of reporting arise. Indeed, the newsroom was a female-free zone – deliberately. Nor had I ever considered that I should ever venture within. In those days journalism still had that air of smoke-wreathed mystery – a trade that evolved in obscure weekly newspapers, plied by blokes fluent in the language of police canteens, dog-tracks and meetings of council highways and byways committees. However, when absolutely desperate, the fraternity of the newsroom would call upon all hands to wield a microphone. And so I occasionally found myself cast in the role of news reporter. And, horribly early in such a role, I learned that not all that I observed and heard necessarily got transmitted. The lessons were random and varied.

I found myself heading one morning towards a small village in County Durham. An excited voice had called our newsroom, and the word 'murder' had been used. As I parked the radio car at the end of a row of terraced houses, I wondered how one went about 'making enquiries', as it were. I'd no idea where to start. I shouldn't have worried. As I emerged with a microphone and tape-recorder a small crowd hurtled round the corner. Far from being reticent, they all had their two-penn'orth to add. I settled on a confident-looking man and asked 'What happened?' There followed a detailed and very vivid description of an age-old story. Husband says good-bye to wife and goes off to work. Several neighbours see this. Shortly afterwards another man enters the house. Neighbours' curtains twitch. Shortly after that, husband, having forgotten snack-box, returns. Ructions ensue. Entire village, it would seem, witnesses naked man pursued through cabbages in nearby allotments by husband with bread-knife, with fatal consequence among the prize leeks. I was mesmerized and taped every detail.

No – I Haven't Got News For You

Back at the radio station, I edited the tape and prepared to go on air, when a more seasoned reporter had a listen. He turned to me and said, 'It's not usual to start a murder report with a detailed portrait of the man who dunnit, including his name and a lurid picture of his personal habits, while the police – as you say – are still looking for him.'

I have no formal training as a journalist – perhaps a statement of the blindingly obvious. I have learned my trade through hard experience, and am much indebted to more senior colleagues who have ensured, especially in the early days, that I have been pulled back from libel, slander, and contempt of court, in my initial naïve assumption that I could bring you all of the news. My observations are those of one who is privileged to work as a news reporter – one who has got away with it for quite a long time. And they are just that – observations, not judgements – for that is the nature of what I do.

Media Freedom?

The idea that journalists have complete freedom to say what they like is, of course, a fallacy. There are many limitations and restrictions, apart from the obvious legal prohibitions. Curiously, I find though that the greatest limitations are self-imposed. The media themselves are the ones who withhold and curtail information. I say curiously, because the general assumption, particularly among young people, is that it is government that wields the scissors of censorship. This is undeniably true in

3

those traditional areas of contention – national security and the business of government. Ludicrous secrecy and evasion still holds sway. If I were to divulge to you the number of socks ordered by the army this year, then all of us would be in trouble. Compared to other modern Western democracies, we British have a poor record in candour and openness. Every party in opposition has pledged to clean the murky window for us to see how our own society functions. Once in office, however, every government has gleefully grabbed the keys to the secret files and thought up a whole new way of keeping those secrets locked away.

We British resemble a dwarf sitting on a supposed pile of treasure in a darkened dungeon, fearful lest anyone other than another privileged dwarf should even acknowledge that such a treasure exists. Knowledge is power. We have had absurd scenarios for years – and continue to have them – in which information freely available abroad has been declared non-existent, invisible and certainly not available. Adult citizens are treated as irresponsible children, and the media are tentative and frequently lazy in challenging the power of the executive and arcane laws which are an affront to responsible citizens.

I was once detained by the authorities, as they say, for filming the front gate of the Atomic Energy Research Establishment at Harwell. A bus was passing at the time.

'You cannot film – it's forbidden,' I was told. 'Why?' I asked. Solemnly, I was informed that a Soviet spy might see our film on the television. 'What if there's a Soviet spy on that bus?' I persisted. 'He might not guess what the place is,' came the reply. 'Why bother to guess,' I said, 'seeing there's a large notice board next to the gate, saying Atomic Energy Research Establishment.' The exchange took off into realms that Kafka would have recognized, involving Russian-speaking bus passengers queuing up in Newbury, and the number of Soviet spies watching the BBC 6 o'clock news. All mildly amusing, except for the fact that some people take this sort of thing to be the cutting edge of national security, and the BBC got a hefty complaint.

Absurd and risible at times, national security is nevertheless used as a catch-all phrase to absolve governments of the need to explain and the obligation to inform demoratic citizens. Government business as well is still frequently hidden behind convenient and obstructive rules, backed by an attitude which *prefers* secrecy and displays a contempt for an enquiring public, and not only at the highest level. Many local councils sneak off into private session, using the excuse of commercial confidentiality – with the public suspicious that deals are being done, and with a local press only occasionally ready to take a tin opener to this particular can of worms. Investigative journalism is time-consuming, expensive, and politically prickly. And nothing like as popular with editors – and proprietors – as is fondly assumed.

However, those areas are not my usual beat, though I realise that a great number of decisions about openness and accountability flow in this country from a starting point not of what little shall we hold back, or restrict, but of how much shall we allow them to know. My curiosity,

5

however, is concentrated on what we journalists ourselves decide to hold back, when there is no law to
restrain us.

War Correspondence

In the last ten years or so, I've spent a good deal of time
reporting conflict in its varying forms: wars, civil distur-
bances, revolution, terrorism. The objective of a reporter,
as I see it, is to seek out and verify the facts, and inform
others with all possible speed. The moment, though, that
such reporting involves matters of life and death, a number of problems arise for the seeker after facts. Not that
conflict and warfare live in a unique and isolated world –
it's just that the extremes encountered at times of war
make the usual reporting dilemmas stark and unavoidable. The moment the words 'ourselves' and 'them, the
enemy' are used, reporters are faced with interesting
choices: Are we involved? Or, as journalists – international journalists no less – are we intending to uphold
some lofty, but rather vague, tradition of objectivity, of
independence?

Let me, at this point, mention that the phrase 'international journalist' is not what it seems. It's bandied about,
with the suggestion that borders and flags and allegiances
are nothing to such creatures, who are perceived as having
some kind of world-view – an 'internationalist' status.
Not so. Someone pays the journalist's wages – a business,
a company, an organization, which has its roots firmly in
a particular country. Television companies, in particu-

lar, have national allegiances, whatever their spread and reach. The BBC is British – World Service and all. CNN International is very much an American concept, maybe specifically an Atlanta concept. The main international news agencies, which these days supply the majority of the world's TV news with foreign footage, have either British or American roots. The growing Arab language market reflects an almost exclusive view of events in Jerusalem and the West Bank. And in Russia the fight has been going on since the end of the Communist Empire about just how controlled – or independent – the Russian media are to be. And it's a violent struggle, which has claimed lives. The term 'international journalist' in effect means someone who spends a lot of time in airports, while mislaying laundry in different capital cities.

So, when the cry goes up, 'ourselves' and 'the enemy', the journalist has no refuge in the cloak of international observer and begins to become involved. If your own country declares war – and there's no 'if' when territorial integrity is at stake – then you are confronted with questions of loyalty. This may have already been decided for you, if your newspaper proprietor has been urging the government on. However, for those of us in public service broadcasting, and those journalists jealous of their status as independent monitors of events, it comes as a shock to realise that your hitherto detached position has suddenly shifted. Words that formerly lived for you in history books acquire sharp relevance: patriotism, loyalty. When I put these terms to young students they react with giggling embarrassment – how quaint, they say. They

Kate Adie

seem unaware of the examples in their own lifetimes, such as that of the Bosnian reporters risking death on a daily basis in Sarajevo to print the only paper available in the city during its near-siege – a paper wedded to Bosnian national survival. Equally, the students are unaware of Belgrade journalists, fired with Serbian patriotism, who have never wavered in their attachment to their nation, regardless of the flaws in the regime. Or the Croat press, enthusiastically pumping out Croatian nationalist propaganda from Zagreb. Loyalty, patriotism, nationalism – noble and necessary in the eyes of one side, and seen as biased, inaccurate and prejudiced by the other. No journalist is immune. Trumpets of war sweep away discretion and balance. Whether you call them 'the troops' or 'our boys', questions arise about how much you say about what they're doing – and how much you do not say.

Advances in technology mean that news has the potential to wing its way around the globe in a matter of seconds. And satellites, the basis of this revolution, are unlikely to cease operating during war, because they carry vital military, economic and essential international telecommunications. These satellites now enable TV, radio, print and photographs to move at extraordinary speed.

Sitting at home, the audience is relatively indifferent to the electronic revolution. But news now is a messenger with digitally-winged feet. To give but one example, on board the USS Gonzales in the Adriatic last year, we found ourselves landing by helicopter in order to be told that the ship was launching Cruise missiles within the hour – huge, lethal rockets, contained in rows of pods, fore and aft across the deck. We stood at an alarmingly close distance at the ship's bow, in the dark, and the first missile exploded out of the pod, its rockets kicking in a few feet above us. A frightening, awesome sight. Next to us a photographer from the *New York Times* clicked away, then went immediately below. He attached his camera to his computer, and the picture popped up on screen to be cropped and captioned. He then attached a satellite phone to the computer, dialled, pressed a key, and the picture was embedded in the electronic lay-out on the front page of the *New York Times* – even before the missile reached its target.

Television cameras – previously film cameras – have been going on to battle-fields for most of the last century. But now they have other bits of equipment attached – small satellite dishes, which mean live TV pictures are possible. This has only happened in the last decade, beginning in the Gulf War. This raises the possibility of showing armies preparing for battle, moving into posi-tion, manoeuvring – either live or perhaps a few minutes later – as long as the little satellite dish is nearby. Some companies are concentrating on developing cameras with back-packs which will have a little aerial so that, as the cameraman walks around, the picture is being seen the other side of the world – and not just on land. Two years ago we successfully transmitted live pictures from the deck of HMS Invincible, while Harrier aircraft fighter planes were operational over southern Iraq. We could have transmitted the take-offs live, but we didn't.

9

The satellite business is promiscuous. The pictures can visit TV stations and receiver dishes anywhere in the world. Including Baghdad. And even though we had not declared war against Saddam Hussein, we'd got ourselves involved in the problem of 'ourselves' and 'the enemy'.

We censored ourselves. We withheld immediate pictures of the Harriers heading off over southern Iraq – and in the tradition of my colleague, Brian Hanrahan, during the Falklands War (again undeclared) we waited until we had counted them all back. What motivated us – patriotism? Or was it a fundamental precept that journalists may not be responsible for causing loss of life, or injury? It was nothing written in the rule-books though – just a moral assumption. However, for every life we are safe-guarding on our side, we may well be adding to the threat to 'them', those on the other side, at the receiving end. So, indirectly, you have discounted the responsibility for the lives of 'them' – and you have broken your little moral rule. And while we're fretting about the impact of *our* pictures, who is to say that the other side have not managed to secrete a camera somewhere on shore, or on a passing cargo carrier, watching HMS Invincible launch her Harriers, and are sending those pictures live to Baghdad in order to give due warning to the Iraqis?

Rapid Communication

Or consider the proliferation of mobile phones. Reporters with immediate access to the airwaves can now perch themselves in concealed positions to comment freely on the tactics of a unit of soldiers. They can alert the world to a column of vehicles creeping across a landscape. Or inform a town's radio station that the invaders are on their way. The only thing to hold back this flood of instant information is the individual reporter's decision to censor him or herself. There is, of course, one other means of preventing the news going out – killing the reporter – and there is no doubt, when confronting the rising graph of journalists killed on assignment in the last decade, that many have lost their lives because the military, or those with guns – warlords, militias, armed gangs, mafias – have begun to fear the very presence of the media, hostile or friendly. Traditional battlefield secrecy is in tatters, punctured by the beep of the mobile phone. And the activities of the media are now a major preoccupation of the military, and of the general public. We feel safe and at peace, and we watch the more dangerous events merely through a screen. And we have got used to seeing things very shortly after they have happened and, increasingly, as they happen live. So there is little tolerance in the audience of waiting for material to be vetted, to be cleared. Witness the irritation with NATO last year as pictures were withheld of bombing raids, while it was said 'evaluation and analysis' was in progress. And because the issues were not clear cut, as is now frequently the case when troops are deployed into a conflict in which we have no primary role – the Gulf, the Balkans, East Timor – there's also a considerable angst displayed by the public, a suspicion that delay equates to conceal-ment, obfuscation and deviousness.

And is it just the military who are holding back? Are the media involved in that activity that I've described, of self-censorship, or of trying to work out which information might harm 'ourselves' or be of benefit to 'them'? Indeed, as we stood watching bombers fly from Gioia de Colle in southern Italy last year, heading for Serbia and Kosovo, there was considerable muddle as to whether we should release the information of our own eyes – number of planes out, number back, bombs returned or bombs away – or wait for the slow response of NATO with the official version of events. Or does it not matter one whit – because a Serb in a local café down the road is probably making a couple of calls on his mobile phone? And, if we hear – as journalists do who are doing their job – that bombs are missing their targets, that weather conditions may hamper operations for the next couple of nights, do we make this public – or do we hold back?

The speed of communication is beginning to call into question the conventional – shall we say – 'decent interval' which used to elapse before acknowledgement of significant events. And the fuzzy intentions which characterize intervention in conflicts which do not constitute a direct threat to our own nation – they too call into question the extent to which we feel it is a conflict of 'us' and 'them'.

Censoring Reality

So what is the overriding principle by which we operate

– concern for life, but with exceptions; patriotism; fear of offending a government; or mere laziness, accepting official statements as adequate, and abandoning enquiry? What is certain is that in the future all military operations and armed conflicts covered by the well-equipped media will be subject to increasing argument about what is to be shown and what is to be held back. And central to what is shown is the exact and real nature of conflict. Here, too, there are pitfalls for the TV reporter.

Last year, gathered on the borders of Macedonia, just prior to the NATO move into Kosovo, were a party of journalists. About 15,000 troops were in readiness – so were over 3,500 journalists. This horde – the press, not the military – represents the growing affluence of western media, characterized by an explosion of TV and radio channels, an increased access to cheap printing, and a stream of young people fresh out of the fashionable media studies courses. In countries which have been blessed with peace for over half a century, there's a noticeable trend for aspiring journalists to regard war as the field in which to win their spurs. The conflict in Croatia and Serbia in the early 90s was marked by the arrival of large numbers of foreign freelancers – young and armed with a notebook and high street camera, who for the price of a train ticket had been able to get to a theatre of war, just a few hours from most western European capitals. The first months of that conflict were also marked by a string of incidents, in which these young hopefuls were caught in crossfire, trod on mines, and ran into trouble generally.

Now it's often been the case in the last 150 years that

war has been the proving ground for the press, but there seem to be two new factors. First, the sheer numbers involved, almost rivalling the military strength – and, second, the innocence of those who are so keen to 'see some action'. Indeed, I've lost count of the number of bright-eyed students whose only ambition is to be a 'war correspondent'. What *do* they think they're going into? Coddled in peaceful countries, a generation or more away from family experience of war and fed on a diet of Hollywood fantasy, where heroes win, bullets cause a minor twinge of pain and violence is explicable, they have yet to grasp the reality of war. And how can that be, when so much war has featured on television news? So much – but only so much, for we bring you an edited version. It is edited not only in terms of withholding information, but in terms of the very nature of war: violence – edited; suffering – only up to a point; cruelty – limited; torture – never. The dreadful face of war is veiled on the TV screen.

The reasons are not difficult to discern, but the degree to which the editing and filtering process occurs is much more debatable. The arbitrary nine o'clock watershed policy means that reality is toned down considerably before nine. The fact that those children most vulnerable to disturbing influence are likely to be viewing unsupervised after nine is part of the arbitrariness. But, even after the watershed, there is never the full picture of conflict these days. Standards of taste, decency, and cultural acceptance come into play. Here is a rulebook that can never be successfully written. It is more a rule-of-thumb applied with experience. The first people to consider what might be recorded – or not – are myself and the cameraman or woman.

Uzdol, a village in Bosnia 1992 – across the fields on a late summer's morning are scattered bodies. Others are in the silent houses, some still in their beds. It is a massacre of over thirty people. All, except one child, are over sixty. We stay our distance. Experience teaches us to take pictures from doorways, or across the fields. Close-ups are not acceptable on British television. The grieving relatives who are with us are affronted. They accuse us of shying away from recording the truth. They want everything on camera, in detail, from blood-soaked walls to individual outrages. We know that this kind of image is not shown on British television. But later, having carefully edited the story, we are told from London that it is still unacceptable for an early evening news audience. A programme editor objects to the very suggestion of a corpse in shot, and a re-edited version just makes it on to the nine o'clock news. However, every trace of the nastiness of war has had to be argued for, and deaths of nearly three dozen people are made to seem tidy and distant.

These editorial attitudes have arrived in the last decade. And they are accompanied by an increasingly emotional reaction to the hard facts of life, which substitutes the sentimental for the raw emotion, and seeks to empathize rather than report and explain. Pictures that were acceptable during the Vietnam war and the 70s in Northern Ireland are now deemed by some to be untransmittable. To extract an official reason why is difficult. At best, there are woolly arguments, backed by not a shred of academic or statistical evidence, that 'society's tolerance has changed'. But it's much more likely that TV companies have grown less confident in putting unacceptable scenes before the public. Troubling pictures mean trouble from politicians and public figures. Well-tested arguments in defence of contentious journalism are eschewed in favour of quiet accommodation. The will to justify showing unpleasant reality grows weaker in an atmosphere which sees the media as an entertainment industry, where corporate values oust editorial judgement. So, have we got tidied-up news for you.

I'm not advocating that all the horrors should be thrust on screen – you must not lose viewers' trust by terrorizing them – but it's becoming ever more difficult to convey the basic nature of conflict properly. The net result is that television makes a dreadful war into a spectator sport. This makes it even harder to understand *why* conflict occurs, and why it drags on. The hatred and violence is rendered meaningless – viewers shake heads, saying 'How stupid can these people be?' Sympathy and interest are lost. And the bright young things head off to report war, believing it to be a *bit* unpleasant, but with no concept of hell on earth, nor of the arguments about what should and should not be told.

Democracy and Truth

There is one significant area which often occurs in war – but not exclusively – which constitutes a nightmare in holding back information – hostage-taking. With the underlying precept that the media may not endanger life, the hostage-takers indulge in every kind of manipulation, and so do the negotiators – families, governments, companies, the police. All reporters, myself included, have watched as lies have been publicly peddled and felt powerless to gainsay them. Meanwhile, governments – as in Beirut in the 80s – deny any involvement, while their agents scuttle past the press bearing messages and ransoms. Or families do deals, all the while threatening journalists, reminding them that a word of the truth could cause death.

Keeping reality off the screen can cause bizarre moments. Some time ago I learned that burials appear to have entered the no-go area for cameras. The very opposite of early days in Belfast, when tough news editors judged some funerals to be very much part of the political process. After all, the average funeral tends not to have balaclava'd people nipping out from behind gravestones to fire shots in the air, thus causing on one occasion a nervous and unsuspecting foreign cameraman to pitch forward into the grave ahead of the coffin. The deceased's family took umbrage, declaring that 'himself wasn't going into any grave already used'. And they marched back home with the coffin. Under today's new sensitivities, I'm not sure how we would explain the coffin's abrupt departure homeward. However, one of the present arguments is that such an event is a 'private occasion' and that reporters must withdraw. For, in matters of grief there is increasing reticence, replacing private sorrow with bunches of flowers and sentimental shrines of toys and messages – which are intentionally placed very publicly alongside, it must be said, personal details of private lives. The raw emotion surrounding death may be off limits, but open season has been declared by many in the media on private lives. A torrent of gossip, titillation, disclosures, revelations – often laced with a strong taste of *schadenfreude* – cascades through our media, in many areas displacing the complex concerns of the world's poor and besieged. To many people it would seem that the media have no rules whatsoever about holding back with regard to the intimate and the personal. The pressures of an entertainment-led culture, allied with a personality-driven public life, deliver a parade of trivial stories where no rules or ethical restraint is evident.

It is not a clear picture then. We withhold the serious and life-threatening, but are under increasing pressure to deliver instant information. We avoid the realities of conflict, especially pain, and deliver reassuring sentimental images. We shudder at private grief, but lap up tales from the bedroom. And, in this, the reporter tries to find a set of rules to work to – impossible, of course. But people like me are helped by a lively debate, an awareness of what freedom of information means, and a sense that the audience is interested in what is reported – and what is not. And I believe it's important that those editorially in charge of the media make their decision-making process public, and are accountable for decisions when information is withheld. A better-informed public makes for a healthier democracy. There may be times when we are compelled to admit that *we do not have news for you*, but we should always be ready to explain and to justify those rare occasions.

'The Long March?' – Whitehall and Open Government since 1945

PETER HENNESSY

History and Journalism

My theme binds Government with the two professional
worlds I have occupied over very nearly the last 30 years
– journalism and the teaching of history. The link with
my time as a Whitehall correspondent is plain enough.
But what about the academic world to which I returned
full-time eight years ago? Well, the pursuit of contemporary British history is powerfully influenced by the public
records policies pursued by successive governments
which determine the release of formerly highly classified
material after 30 years and by the attitudes of prime
ministers and cabinets towards open or closed government for current and very recent information. Back, for
a moment then, to my twin jobs. When pondering a new
piece, historians begin by reaching for the founding file
in the archive; journalists start by hunting for the first
good story from behind the scenes. May I open with an
episode that satisfies the joint cravings which flow from

these two streams of my professional life? Come with me to Mr Attlee's No. 10 Downing Street and the Cabinet Office in the spring of 1946 and let us reconstruct the first really serious Whitehall leak enquiry of the post-war years. What ghastly breach of security had triggered it?

Two related pieces on the future of the iron and steel industry appeared in *The Times* of 25 March 1946. The paper's 'City Notes' of that day, rather than the news story filed by its Parliamentary Correspondent (anonymous as all *Times* people were until 1966), gives the flavour of the item and the special offence it caused within Government circles.

The 'intro' itself has a wonderful period flavour: 'The question whether the iron and steel industry is to be nationalized or not came up to the Cabinet for discussion for the first time on Thursday. It may thus be an appropriate moment to review the progress of this controversial question.'[1] Quite so – John Wilmot, the Minister of Supply, had drawn up a paper on the pros and cons which, said *The Times*, 'reported generally in favour of nationalization. This report came before the special Cabinet economic sub-committee presided over by Mr (Herbert) Morrison (Lord President of the Council) . . . Mr Morrison's committee, presumably finding itself in some uncertainty, neither endorsed nor rejected Mr Wilmot's report. The whole question was, it is understood, passed up to the Cabinet itself for decision without prejudice and without recommendation.'[2]

The secret and sacred world of the Cabinet committee system had been breached. Sir Norman Brook, the formidable Secretary of the Cabinet, swung into action and he set off from Whitehall to Printing House Square in Blackfriars to confront the Editor of *The Times* personally with his affront to the interests of the state and good (i.e. private) government. As Brook reported later to the Prime Minister, Clem Attlee:

> Mr Barrington Ward was in Germany when the article was published and I went to see him on 1st April, the first day after his return to London. I told him that I had come on my own initiative and not at the suggestion of Ministers: that I had not come to ask from whom the information had been obtained: but I had thought it wrong to let this article pass without letting him know that we, as officials serving the Cabinet, thought that the publication in the Press of such details of Cabinet organisation (the membership of particular committees, which Ministers had attended a particular meeting, etc.) were a hindrance to the efficient discharge of public business.[3]

And how did the Editor of *The Times* react? Did he run through his head the words penned in 1852 by John Thaddeus Delane, his fabled predecessor in the Editor's chair, which declared that: 'The Duty of the journalist is the same as that of the historian – to seek out the truth, above all things, and to present to his readers not such things as statecraft would wish them to know but the truth as near as he can attain it.'[4]

No, he did not. Far from politely telling the Cabinet

Secretary to push off, Barrington Ward, as Brook put it: '. . . appreciated my point and agreed that "there were things which were necessary to the news and things which were not." Would I leave it to him to look into the matter? I said that, having made my comment, I was quite content to leave it at that.'[5] Days of innocence and deference. Whitehall, however, did not leave the matter there. The Lord Chancellor, no less, conducted a leak enquiry at the Cabinet's request.[6] Lord Jowett found strong grounds for believing that *The Times* article '. . . was based on information derived, either directly or indirectly, from officials in the Ministry of Supply who were familiar with the course of the ministerial discussions on the subject. But the relations between the Ministry of Supply and the Iron and Steel Federation are necessarily so close that it is not surprising that some information reached the Press.' As a result, the Lord Chancellor advised the Prime Minister there should be no recourse to a prosecution under the Official Secrets Act.[7]

The file ends with a brisk, Attlee-style Cabinet paper on 'Leakage of Information' stating that the Lord Chancellor would investigate on his behalf 'all future cases of apparent leakage of official information regarding matters under discussion by the Cabinet or its Committees'.[8]

Opening the Secret Garden

Thanks to John Major's decision in 1992 both to publish the terms of reference and the membership of ministerial

Cabinet committees *and* the ministerial rulebook *Questions of Procedure for Ministers,*[9] it is difficult to appreciate fully nowadays the lengths to which ministers and officials went to preserve their 'secret garden' of a Cabinet system in the early post-war years. Just listen to this passage from the first Attleean consolidated version of *Questions of Procedure*: 'The underlying principle is, of course, that the method adopted by Ministers for discussion among themselves of questions of policy is essentially a domestic matter, and is no concern of Parliament or the public.'[10]

Note that 'of course'. These truths were held to be self-evident. And that form of words survived as late as the 1966 version of *QPM*.[11] Even when I began operating as a Whitehall correspondent in the mid-1970s, the principle of complete privacy of process (let alone content) continued to be asserted. Jim Callaghan's 1976 edition of *QPM*, for example, declared that 'the method adopted by Ministers for discussing among themselves questions of policy is essentially a domestic matter and such discussion will be hampered if the process by which it is carried on is laid bare.'[12]

Jim Callaghan, who I always respected and came to like very much, authorized more than one leak enquiry into my activities when I blew a scattering of his Cabinet committees and ministerial groups. They were normally conducted by a very decent, old fashioned chap, the late Basil Lock, the Cabinet Office's security man. He was a former airman who had run RAF Coastal Command. I had his photograph above my desk in *The Times* building in order, as it were, that he could keep an eye on what I was doing. He never caught one of my helpers. I would usually be leaked the result of his leak inquiries. I grew rather fond of him at a distance. And if for some reason he was not assigned to one of my leak inquiries, I used to make discreet inquiries after his health.

We have come a long way in 25 years. As I sat down to write this paper I had before me a copy of the January 2000 edition of the Cabinet Office's Guide to Departments on 'Cabinet Committee Business' – now a quite open document which lists all of Mr Blair's ministerial Cabinet committees and gives you the contact name and number of the Cabinet Office official who services them.[13] In the late 1970s and early 1980s Bruce Page and I used to work ourselves to the bone to extract and publish stuff like this.[14]

It would be misleading to suggest that the British press, even its more investigative arms, had pushed hard or consistently throughout the post-war period against what Jimmy Margach of *The Sunday Times* once called 'the walls of Whitehall's forbidden city.'[15] With a few brave exceptions, the late 1940s and the 1950s saw a depressing spread of the disease of lobbyitis which took root in Westminster in the 1880s when political journalists first organized themselves into a group of lobby correspondents.[16]

Francis Williams, the former Editor of the *Daily Herald* who went into No. 10 with Attlee as his Press Secretary, was eloquently and critically accurate about this in his long-forgotten book, *Parliament, Press and the Public*, which was published in 1946. Williams had worked in the Ministry of Information during World War II and watched with dismay as the lobby contagion spread to other groups of specialist journalists. By the end of the war, he wrote, it was:

> ... normal practice for some of the big Departments to hold regular background and news conferences with the Press. At these conferences information is sometimes given by the Minister, sometimes by the Public Relations Officer and sometimes by other senior officials of the Ministry. In a number of cases only correspondents belonging to a recognized group, with its own officials and rules, are now invited to these conferences ... It is easy to see the advantages of such a system to a Department.

Williams touched on the ever-present temptation to collude and the price of such collusion:

> Such a system also means that the newspaper correspondents concerned give up much of their independence. Some of them tend to depend so largely on official sources for information and to develop such obligations to the officials with whom they work that they become mouthpieces of authority, taking their 'line' from the Minister ...'

There is nothing new in 'spin'. There were, Williams concluded, people of ability and independent judgement among the press corps who took their own line. But 'their presence does not alter the general principle that anything which ties newspapers too closely to official sources of news, or sets up obligations which may conflict with a newspaper's primary responsibility to the public, is a bad system and ought not to exist.'[17] Amen to all of that. The lobby is now both a much diminished *and* a more transparent phenomenon, but the Williams' critique still has bite in terms of the turn-of-the-century version of a dependency culture in which the spinners and the spun currently operate.

No. 10 press people in any generation rarely relish the awkward squad who rub up against the cosy and the collusive. Just listen to this brief provided for Attlee's successor in No. 10, Winston Churchill, in the autumn of 1954. At issue was the question of which minister should be the regular briefer of the lobby correspondents, Lord Swinton or the Chancellor of the Exchequer, Rab Butler. Such things were way beneath the ken of the Prime Minister who preferred to deal with the Press Lords directly rather than dally with any jobbing journalist.

As a result, an idiot's brief on lobby practice had to be prepared for the grand old man by Fife Clark, Director-General of the Central Office of Information, into which the Ministry of Information had mutated at the end of the war. Swinton, Fife Clark told Churchill, had been the Lobby correspondents' 'friend and advocate for two and a half years and the Lobby are very grateful to him, just as they have become very fond of him personally. Their gratitude has been expressed not once but many times in the secrecy of the Lobby Room.'[18] This is more masonry than journalism. 'Three years ago,' Clark continued, 'ministers were not so sure that they could trust the lobby. Now they know they can.' There was, however, a minority among the ranks of the Lobby correspondents who sullied this cloying scene. It was, wrote Clark, 'headed by Derek Marks and Robert Carvel of the *Daily Express*, but it is fair to say that this group is dissident on most issues and it would not be easy for any Minister to provide them, week in week out, storm or calm, with all the news they think they ought to have.'[19] There you have it – the expectation of a master/mendicant relationship which only the rough trade on the Beaverbrook press was cut up about. Not the slightest trace of Delane's dictum there, let alone more modern notions of a right to know.

In fact, it took another half-generation before White-hall began to address the possibility that there might be a case for substantially greater press and public access to official information. The declassified records suggest that it needed the 1968 Fulton Report on the Civil Service, and the glancing blow it struck in the twentieth of its twenty-two recommendations suggesting a further enquiry was needed into 'ways and means of getting rid of unnecessary secrecy both in policy-making and administration',[20] to provide the momentum for an examination of the virtues and the perils of a deliberately created increase in openness.

Beginnings of Openness

The first post-Fulton stab at an openness policy has been generally overlooked during the thirty or so years since, partly because it resulted in a truly feeble White Paper, *Information and the Public Interest*, published in June 1969. This concluded lamely that 'There would be the greatest difficulty in defining satisfactorily what categories of information should qualify for . . . Special protection and what should not'[21], adding the breathtakingly complacent gloss that the public and Parliament should not be worried about the Official Secrets Acts as they did not 'inhibit the authorized release of information in any way'.[22] *Information and the Public Interest* swiftly became overshadowed by the intellectually robust and impressively coherent Franks Report on Section 2 of the Official Secrets Act commissioned by the Heath Government in 1971, which was published in 1972[23] and eventually formed the basis of the narrower, more defensible, Official Secrets Act of 1989.[24]

Harold Wilson's No. 10 file which traces the road from Fulton to the mouse of a White Paper a year later, was declassified in January 2000.[25] It turned out to be a revealing little gem on what, following Robinson and Gallagher's terminology, might be called the 'official mind'[26] of official secrecy. Wilson, to his credit, combined in a bizarre fashion an opener's temperament with a paranoia about leaks to which the Public Record Office files frequently and vividly attest.[27] Yet, without his personal insistence, it is most unlikely that the 50-Year Rule would have been reduced to 30 by the Public Records Act, 1967.[28] In this sense, Wilson could be called the political patron of the boom in contemporary British history which has resounded with increasing resonance since the 30-Year Rule came into force in 1972, not least thanks to the press attention new batches of files now routinely attract when made available at the Public Record Office in Kew.

Initially post-Fulton, Wilson 'had doubted whether there would in fact be much of a demand for a renew of the [Official Secrets] Acts'[29] but he had been struck by a speech delivered by Ted Heath, then Leader of the Opposition, at the Granada Press Awards in January 1969 (during which Heath pledged that once elected his Government would review existing official secrets legislation as 'politicians should make it possible for the media to improve the level of political discussion by reducing and eliminating the obstacles that stand in their way'.[30] Never one to be outbid by the competition, Wilson declared in a speech a week or so later during a dinner in the Savoy to celebrate the 50th anniversary of the *Sunday Express* that following the Fulton recommendation, 'the whole question of the release of official information, including the Official Secrets Act, should now be under consideration'.[31]

All sorts of grand people were considered for the chairmanship of a committee of enquiry into secrecy. Wilson suggested the former Labour minister, Bert Bowden (by this stage ennobled as Lord Aylestone)[32] but his Principal Private Secretary, Michael Halls, cautioned against this since Aylestone had left politics to run ITV: 'he might well come out with far too liberally-minded a report – almost Swedish,' declared Halls, as if such a thing was both inconceivable and deeply shocking in a British context.[33]

The senior Civil Service, not just Halls, were, in fact, truly alarmed by the possibilities an enquiry might open up. The two great figures of the late 1960s Whitehall – the Cabinet Secretary, Sir Burke Trend, and the Head of the Home Civil Service, Sir William Armstrong – weighed in with a beautifully-crafted brief for the Prime Minister and the Cabinet perfectly designed to make ministerial flesh creep, which moved from one classic fallback position to the next. Just listen to this:

> The Prime Minister may wish to draw the Cabinet's attention to the two broad categories of information which are likely to be at issue in this enquiry. The first category consists of factual and statistical information; the chief limitations on the release of more information of this sort are how far there is a real public demand for it and how far Civil Service numbers can be increased to cope with the work of preparing it for publication.[34]

Fallback number one: nobody really wants it and it'll cost a lost of money if we do it. There's more: 'There is likely to be much greater public interest in the second broad category of information – the stuff of which policy decisions are made.'[35] Tricky this – there's evidence here of public demand. Don't worry. Fallback number two takes care of this one. We're satisfying that already: 'By the Green Paper approach, the Government have [sic] extended the process of public consultation . . . And this process is likely to continue.'[36]

Now the *coup de grâce*. Fallback number three is deployed – go directly for Ministers' neuroses:

Many policy decisions, however, are based not only on an assessment of measurable factors but also on a number of subjective judgements on questions such as the influence of other commitments and the reactions of various interests at home and abroad. The publication of a full analysis of the considerations involved in a policy decision may not be practicable or expedient in every case. For example, would Ministers have wished to publish such analysis in advance of the decision to go ahead with the development of the Concorde project: or would they now wish to commit themselves to do so in advance of a decision whether to put Concorde into full production?[37]

This cascade of fallbackery has a malign beauty about it. It's an art form.

As always with the best Whitehall breeds, a way out is suggested. And it turned on what the journalist James Cameron once called 'the defence of the face':[38]

An outside enquiry may well produce general recommendations which, if accepted, could restrict the Government's freedom in the process of decision making. Since, however, it seems necessary to meet the public demand for such an enquiry, it is desirable to frame its terms of reference in such a way as to minimise, so far as is possible, the risk of embarrassment.[39]

This is beyond parody. You could not make it up without risk of being accused of exaggeration. In the event, there was no enquiry, no embarrassing report. The Inner Cabinet ruled it out.[40] That inside job – the puny White Paper – was its surrogate.

Freedom of Information?

In 1969, the internal debate was all about the loss of control – and it still is as 31 years later, an emasculated and wrongly-named Freedom of Information Bill goes through its last Parliamentary stages. Wrongly named? How can that be? Because FOI and open government are two different things. As Robert Hazell told the House of Commons Public Administrations Committee in 1999:

> The Government still does not fully understand the difference between open government and freedom of information. Open government means the Government publishing information largely for its own purposes: information that the Government thinks we need to know or might like to know. Freedom of information requires the Government to disclose information which we decide for ourselves we want to know.[41]

The distinction has never been better put. The Prime Minister, Tony Blair, does not understand this distinction but that's not altogether surprising as he doesn't believe in open government for the Cabinet let alone for the public. But the Home Secretary of the day, Jack

Straw, *did* understand the Hazell distinction. For he admitted privately to the view that 'Freedom of information is for oppositions not for governments' adding that 'open government is for governments'.[42] So, as a journalist-turned historian on an awards evening, to which post-war premiers would I grant an openness, if not a freedom of information, prize?

Third place goes to Ted Heath for commissioning the Franks report which showed that the limits to official secrecy could be both narrowed and liberalized. Had he been re-elected in 1974, I am pretty confident he would have legislated in a reformist direction. I have always suspected Mrs Thatcher allowed the 1989 legislation to proceed because, with a streamlined secrets law, juries might, when faced with future Clive Pontings, be more readily persuaded to convict. Second place goes to Harold Wilson for the Public Records Act of 1967 and the 30-Year Rule. Think how diminished we historians would be if last January we had eagerly awaited the opening of the 1949 papers rather than those for 1969.

First prize – by a clear margin – goes to John Major. Why? We have already seen how in 1992 he declassified both the ministerial rulebook and the bone structure of the Cabinet committee system. In addition he placed the first properly institutionalized openness regime on a codified, if not a statutory, basis in 1993–94[43] with (again for the first time) someone outside the Whitehall loop having a say in disputed disclosure cases in the person of the Parliamentary Ombudsman.[44] Major also had a sense of delayed open government. He backed his public service minister, William Waldegrave, in his drive to re-review and release, if possible, once highly sensitive documents which had been retained beyond the 30-Year norm. As a result of the so-called 'Waldegrave Initiative' nearly 100,000 files have been released, many of them cold-war related enabling contemporary historians to reconstruct for the first time the secret cold-war state which was grafted on to the existing one from the late 1940s.[45]

There is a symbiotic link between past, present and future here – a need for what the Chief Executive of BP, Lord Browne of Madingly, has called 'accelerated history'[46] – that is, a proper freedom of information regime with ministers only able to keep policy advice and material under wraps within a carefully circumscribed inner ring of genuinely sensitive matters. Without such a regime, as Sir John Hoskyns pointed out nearly twenty years ago, 'there is no learning curve' in the government, the press or the country at large.[47] The same point about transparency, the timely dissemination of knowledge and the indispensability of informed debate was made in 2000 by 'The BSE Enquiry' report published by Lord Philips, Mrs June Bridgeman and Professor Malcolm Ferguson-Smith.[48]

Ted Heath put it splendidly at the Granada Awards Lunch in 1969. 'An open society,' he said, 'is one in which the people, through the press and television, can have ready access to the information on which they can judge policies and policy makers . . . The result of unnecessary secrecy is that it exalts the "informed circle", the off-the-record comment and leak. The manipulation of news takes the place of news-gathering.'[49] How familiar that sounds a generation later. If you believe, as Philip Graham did and I do, that the prime function of quality newspapers is to provide 'the first rough draft of history'[50] such matters as public records and freedom of information policies are central to the two professions in which I have spent my adult working life. Whether the current quality press in Britain even aspires to Philip Graham's gold standard is a different question and the subject for quite another paper.

God, Morals and Secrecy

GERARD J. HUGHES SJ

Introduction

To invite a fully paid-up theist to contribute to a discussion on open government might at least on the face of it seem paradoxical. It is not as though the divine governance of the universe can honestly be said to be an open book, even when read by believers. God's ways are not our ways. To take but one biblical example, Job is told in no uncertain terms that he does not and will not understand what is going on, and has no right to question whatever arrangements God may have made. Moreover, you have invited not merely a theist but a Roman Catholic to contribute; and I would not suppose that the Roman Catholic Church, whatever her many virtues, can be held up as a distinguished example of open government. Perhaps worst of all, I am a Jesuit – and are we Jesuits not notorious for the practice of secrecy, and the theory of equivocation and mental reservation when forced to account for ourselves in tricky situations?

Needless to say, I would not be contributing did I consider these handicaps to be altogether insuperable. Taken together, though, they might suggest in a general

Gerard J. Hughes SJ

kind of way that 'God, Morals, and Secrecy' was a sensible topic for the organizers to choose rather than 'God, Morals and Open Government'. This is the impression that I shall try to dispel.

I wish to address three issues. The first is to explain why it is not altogether surprising that I – and indeed I would say 'we' – do not come from a long tradition of enthusiasm for open government. Secondly, I hope that in explaining why this should be so, I shall throw some light which will help us to assess two frequently proposed arguments in favour of open government. Thirdly, I shall outline the type of consideration which best supports a policy of open government, and show how this case, while not in itself a specifically Christian or theistic case, nevertheless fits well with important elements in the Christian tradition.

Why is the tradition not clearer?

An excellent outline of the legal measures which might constitute an adequate framework for open government is to be found in the Johannesburg Principles, drawn up in 1995 by a group of international jurists.[1] In discussing both freedom of expression and freedom of information, they argue that both these freedoms are vital to democracy, and essential for progress, welfare and the protection of other important rights and freedoms. In so saying they are, I think, advancing the kinds of considerations which would strike many, and perhaps most, of us as exactly the right starting point.

God, Morals and Secrecy

It was not always thus, however. Democracy is indeed a very ancient form of government; but one must admit that it is both ancient and long thought to be discredited. Plato, who had lived through the collapse of the Athenian democracy which had executed Socrates, advocated a benign form of paternalistic oligarchy. He became, in Karl Popper's words, an enemy of the open society. Aristotle, at the end of a long study of the various constitutions in force in his time, did not conclude that democracy was the ideal, though he was less unsympathetic to democracy than Plato. Both would have objected that anything like a modern democracy places government in the hands of the uninformed and unfit; and even with a highly restrictive citizenship-qualification Aristotle is still no out-and-out democrat.

To the extent that Christianity flourished in Europe, it did so against a background either of tribalism, or empire, or monarchy. Its adopted philosophies during a millennium and a half were for the most part those of Plato or Aristotle. Christian practice typically involved elements of monarchy, oligarchy, and (perhaps especially in the religious orders) democracy, if by that is meant a greater devolution of powers. But the value of democracy in itself was hardly an undisputed axiom of government, whether civil or ecclesiastical. If the main argument for freedom of information is that it is vital to the preservation of democracy, such an argument would have seemed to most Christians to be completely and utterly perverse, and its conclusion pointless.

Nor would the argument that open government is

essential for the preservation of human rights have met with much greater success. For while many of the key elements upon which a theory of human rights must rest were in place in ancient times, and were thoroughly defended by canon lawyers in the Middle Ages, the doctrine in its fully explicit form is still a comparative latecomer to Christian tradition. No such rights were discussed in connection with the treatment of Jews, for instance, still less of Turks. The fact that, in the Enlightenment, ideas of democracy and the rights of man were so often associated with revolution and secularism did not exactly help to commend them to Christians.

Thus, in my own Church, tendencies described as 'liberalism' and 'democracy', together with radical theories of human rights were often condemned right up until the third quarter of the nineteenth century, and only gradually and somewhat grudgingly accepted in the following fifty years. Neither the Catholic Church nor its opponents could step back sufficiently far to dissociate democracy from anti-clericalism, or the advocacy of human rights from extreme socialist revolution. Demands for open government would have been widely regarded by various Catholic authorities as threatening and no better than malicious interference. The difference in tone between official Catholic documents from 1850 to 1960 is absolutely enormous. The inference is plain, that the Church throughout this period was reacting desperately and somewhat blindly to political and social pressures rather than responding from the riches of a long-standing and well-assimilated tradition of Christian social teaching. On these topics, such a tradition simply did not exist. But if the legitimacy, and even the desirability of democracy was accepted by the Church only gradually (and even then, only as it might affect civil society), then *a fortiori* there was little question of advocating open government as an essential bulwark of democracy.

Indeed, there were elements in Catholic tradition which told directly against any tendency which might have issued in open government. The most striking of these would be the absolute insistence, in canon law and in universal ecclesiastical practice, of the secrecy of the confessional. This is, of course, a particularly emphatic teaching, and one which in canonical strictness was of very limited application; but it did have a strong influence on the development of the notion of professional confidentiality quite generally. So, if open government were to be argued for by claiming that everyone has a right to the whole truth about anything which might affect them, there was already a strong, and in some instances a sacred tradition which precisely asserted the contrary. In passing, I might call attention to something of a parallel here between the tradition of professional confidentiality almost no matter what, and the clause in the Johannesburg Principles which insists that the media have an absolute legal right to protect the anonymity of their sources.

It may have struck many of you that in discussing some of the reasons for the lack of any strong Christian tradition, and in particular of any strong Catholic tradition, which might have favoured a campaign for open government, I started in the Middle Ages and went on from there. What about the New Testament?

I do not believe that there are any New Testament texts which have any direct bearing on open government. Someone might rather naively try to allege Matthew, 10:27, 'Nothing is covered which will not be revealed, or hidden which will not be made known. What I tell you in darkness, speak in the light, and what you hear whispered, proclaim from the rooftops.' But it takes but a moment's attention to the context to see that Matthew does not take Jesus to be making any general remarks about secrets or confidentiality. He is urging the disciples to fearless confession of their faith, despite the dangers, secure in the knowledge that their father in heaven cares for them. The parallel saying in Mark (4:21–22) occurs in an even more general context, but again is presented as concerned with the spread of the good news, and not at all with issues of secrecy. A second group of texts would, if anything, point in the direction of secrecy rather than openness, in that they contain injunctions on the part of Jesus to those whom he has cured not to tell anyone about what has happened (e.g. 7:36). Whatever the point of what has been called the 'messianic secret' – and I suppose it must have been intended as a way of avoiding naive misinterpretations of Jesus' ministry – it is clear that, if anything, these texts suggest there was no sense of embarrassment at speaking less than the whole truth, if there were good reasons for so doing. In short, we have two sets of texts which are only remotely connected with issues of open government, in so far as they are linked to it at all. And on balance, they tell rather against than in favour of openness.

There is perhaps a more general consideration which might have influenced Christian tradition. The comparison of the Christian community to a body, enlivened with the Spirit of Christ, would tend to foster two moral conclusions: the first is that, since the body is ruled by its head, so the Christian community should also in some sense be monarchic. A second inference might be that Christians should tend towards a communitarian rather than an individualist approach to morality. In this respect it would find the overall approach of Aristotle congenial, in that Aristotle, too, sees the individual as essentially bound up with the community. It is well known that there is, in Aristotle's ethics, no discussion at all of human rights in the way in which that notion is part and parcel of our more recent individualistic Western ethics. Aquinas, much indebted to Aristotle, lays great stress on the *bonum commune*, the well-being of the community as such, to which individual happiness is at least in some ways subordinate. It is on the whole foreign to his view to see the individual as needing defence against the claims of the community.

For all these reasons, then, it is perhaps less surprising that Christian tradition at least for the first 1,500 years says little about individual human rights, and is only partially influenced by what we might think of as democratic principles. I have suggested that the main lines of contemporary argument in favour of open government appeal to its importance in safeguarding individual human rights and the functioning of democratic institutions. These are goals whose explicit promotion comes not from Christian tradition, but from the assumptions and aims of the Enlightenment. They won neither unanimous nor immediate support from mainstream European Christianity, since in many ways they seemed to present more or less of a threat to the established Christian order of things.

Arguments Best Avoided

In some ways, the lack of a clear Christian tradition on the subject of *secrecy* and open government makes things easier, in that we need not feel committed to any particular conclusions in advance, nor to any particular line of argument in defending whatever conclusions we might wish to reach. In this part of my chapter, I wish to call in question the usual arguments which are advanced in favour of open government, which depend on theories of rights, or the value of democracy and democratic accountability.

First, then, I must say something about open government and the notion of *rights*. Let me make it clear that I am very much in favour of open government; what I am criticizing is a particular way of arguing in favour of it. Let me also make it clear that I have no objection whatsoever to speaking of rights, or of human rights. On the contrary, I think it most important to establish and to defend various rights in general, and human rights in particular. My point is that a defence of open government is not best sought in the doctrine of rights, still less of human rights.

My first reason for so saying is a rather general one. The appropriate use of the language of rights is to emphasize the very special nature of the claim which is being made. To appeal to a right is to claim that one has reasons which of their very nature are more important than any other reasons, unless those others also appeal to a right. Rights, in short, 'trump' all other kinds of considerations. Now it is just this feature of rights-claims which makes it tempting to dress up in the language of rights just about any case one wishes to promote. Unfortunately, yielding to this temptation by expanding the rhetoric of rights runs the risk of cheapening the currency. I heard it recently asserted that prisoners have the right to know the name of all the auxiliaries in the prison – the cleaners and the cooks. This right, the argument was, overrides the fears of the auxiliaries that their families might be harassed if their names were known. How anyone would establish the existence of such a right I find it difficult to see. Making the case in terms of rights is designed precisely to circumvent normal moral discussion of the issues at stake. But the force of the appeal to one's rights in the really important issues in which rights truly are involved is seriously undermined if one spreads the rhetoric too thin.

My second reason is specific to this particular case. I am highly sceptical about the prospects of arguing for anything like a right to know the whole truth about everything in which one has an interest. I am not even sure that one could argue that one has a right not to be lied to: and that is a much more restricted claim than the claim to be told the whole truth about everything. If someone has a right to something, it follows, I believe, that it would be *unjust* to that person to refuse to implement that right; it is not enough to show that it would be a good thing to behave in the required way: it must be unjust not to. I cannot here enter into the complexities of theories of justice. It must suffice to appeal to the commonsense notion that it is not in general unjust to refuse to give someone information about a topic in which they have a genuine interest. People have a genuine interest in the financial status of their business competitors; but it need not be in the least unjust for a competitor to refuse to disclose that information to them. All kinds of sales representatives seem to have an interest in discovering my e-mail address, which I have no intention of disclosing. That this refusal is neither unjust nor unfair is sufficient to show that my refusal to disclose the information violates no rights.

If, then, one cannot defend open government by appeal to some general right to information, does the other argument fare any better, that one needs open government in order to defend the basic practices of democracy? I am not convinced that this is the best defence, either, though I think it better than basing one's argument on rights. Churchill's remark, that democracy is the worst form of government except for the various others which have been tried from time to time, is worth remembering, for two reasons. It serves to remind us that

46

democracy is not an end in itself; and to make the point that one might wish to argue in favour of open (or more open) government in countries which are not democracies, and which would be deaf to any appeal based on democratic principles. It just is not obvious that democracy is the best form of government for every society in every stage of its development.

The Basis for Advocating Open Government

I believe it was Bernard Shaw who said that democracy substitutes election by the incompetent many for appointment by the corrupt few. What democracy does not achieve, in any but the very smallest states, is the rule of the people. In practice, most governments, including those which would most value the title of democracies, are either dictatorships or oligarchies. But two key dangers are common to them all: corruption, and the over-protection of the interests of those who have the privileges of power. The point of open government, I suggest, is to ensure at least some measure of transparency, as a means of minimizing both corruption and bureaucratic incompetence.

To minimize corruption and incompetence in government, and in the institutions of society generally, seems to me to be desirable on the grounds that to do so clearly serves the common good. It can be in nobody's interests to be governed in ways which are corrupt or incompetent. Notice that this is not necessarily a matter of injustice. It may be that if a government is corrupt someone is unjustly treated as a result; but it does not at all follow that if a government is incompetent someone will inevitably be treated unjustly. So one can draw the stronger conclusion that incompetence, and perhaps even corruption, need not violate anyone's rights, even though corruption is morally wrong, and incompetence is in a general way undesirable.

Other grounds might also be urged besides those of avoiding incompetence and corruption. For example, one might argue for open government in order to ensure that the policies which a government is publicly committed to following are those which in fact are being followed. Menzies Campbell, as I write, is pursuing the government for information about the quantity of bombs which continue to be dropped on Iraq, and the compatibility of this behaviour with the Government's announced policy of humanitarian protection of the Kurds and the peasants of the Iraqi delta. This, I believe, raises an interesting and difficult point. One might indeed wish to state categorically that duplicity in one's foreign policy is wrong, and that one should be able to force disclosure in order to make sure that such double-dealing does not happen. It does not seem to me that this argument is conclusive. Firstly, it seems to me no more self-evident in public affairs than it is in individual ethics that there is any *general* requirement to tell the whole truth. Secondly, neither am I convinced that it is always wrong to lie – by which I mean, it is not always wrong to tell an untruth. I note that the recent *Catechism of the Catholic Church*, not the most radical of documents, sidesteps this issue by defining a lie as 'to speak against the truth in order to lead into error someone *who has a right to the truth*'.[2] On either definition of a lie, it will not necessarily be morally wrong to speak an untruth about a nation's foreign policy. I suppose that in particular cases the issue has to be settled in terms of broader considerations about the common good of one's own nation, and the good of the family of nations as a whole.

On general grounds, then, I would argue that open government is perhaps best defended on the basis that it contributes to the common good. In so saying, I can claim *some* support from the Christian tradition. As I have remarked, the biblical images of the Body of Christ, of the Vine, of God as Father of the human family, and of the community formed by the sharing in the eucharist, might provide lines of thought and reflection. In themselves, though, these images do not provide detailed arguments, nor are they suited to the kind of legal discussion which is required if any legal provisions for promoting open government are to be enacted. Of course any attempt to ensure open government by legislation will have to deal with these detailed problems, to which I shall return presently. All I wish to claim at the moment is that an initial approach through these theological images fits well enough with an appeal to philosophical notions such as the *common good*. I prefer to rely on such a notion, indeterminate though to some extent it is, rather than appeal to human rights which are only apparently more clear-cut, and are in any case difficult to defend.

But there is at least one major problem with my

approach. For it can well be objected that I prefer to rely on a notion like the common good rather than on concepts such as rights, or democracy, precisely because the common good is sufficiently vague that it can be made to include or exclude whatever takes one's fancy or appeals to one's prejudices or intuitions. I think this difficulty is a real one, but unavoidable. In a comparatively small society such as Aristotle's it is perhaps more defensible to suppose that the interests of all the citizens will coincide; much as one might try to argue that in a family no one member can live a truly fulfilled life unless the others do so as well. But in larger and more complex societies such as England, or Britain, and still more if we consider the human community as a whole, it is hardly possible to claim that the interests of all human beings coincide. After all, is it not the case that to a considerable extent we in the developed world have managed to cater to our genuine interests by methods which have certainly not been in the interests of millions of our fellow human beings; and, crucially, is it not the case also that we cannot devise ways in which justice can be done without ourselves renouncing some goods and practices which truly are beneficial for us? To be sure, this non-convergence of interests can to some extent be exaggerated. The Hobbesian description of the horrors of the state of nature as a state of constant war with 'the life of man, solitary, poor, nasty, brutish and short' is enough to remind us that there are at least basic features of the common good which are utterly beyond reasonable dispute. Recent or contemporary examples of a Hobbesian state of nature, in the Congo, or Sierra Leone, or Kosovo, or East Timor, are not far to seek. At the other extreme, even Aristotle was prepared to concede that in his small society some people might be called upon to sacrifice their very lives in order to safeguard the interests of their fellow citizens.

The critical usefulness of the concept of the common good should, therefore, be neither exaggerated nor underestimated. In the final section of this lecture, I shall try to show that it is sufficient to give a justification for most of the provisions which one might wish to see enshrined in legislation about open government.

Openness and the Common Good

That in general terms open government serves the common good, while not a truth which we or the founding fathers of the United States might hold to be self-evident, is still a truth which it is comparatively easy to establish. For open government provides what can be an effective check on both incompetence and corruption. And I take it that incompetence and corruption in government simply cannot further the common good. James Madison in a letter written in 1822, said:

> A popular government without popular information, or the means of acquiring it, is but a prologue to a farce or a tragedy, or perhaps both. Knowledge will forever govern ignorance, and a people who mean to be their own governors must arm themselves with the power that knowledge gives.[3]

Madison's argument, as one might expect from an American President, is based on the assumption of the value of democracy, in which the people aim to be their own governors. But the general point does not depend on specifically democratic assumptions. Any form of government which makes no provision for popular information or the means of acquiring it is a prelude either to the farce of unchecked incompetence, or the tragedy of endemic corruption. Once again, evidence is not far to seek. Those who wield political power will inevitably find it in their interests to cover up their mistakes, or to hide their attempts to derive dishonest profit from their position, since such revelations will inevitably weaken the security of their hold over power at least to some extent and in the longer term. Plainly, then, it serves the common good to ensure that such cover-ups can be effectively challenged. It follows that the mere fact that disclosure will cause embarrassment to those in power, or will expose them to possible accusations of misconduct, or will show that they have not been following their stated policies, cannot be acceptable reasons for refusing to divulge the information in question. On the contrary, it can be assumed that requests for disclosure will routinely involve embarrassment or worse; after all, those in power are not normally reticent about disclosing their successes. The legal framework governing disclosure must assume that government will routinely seek to argue that disclosure is undesirable, and must therefore take steps to provide against the misuse of this argument.

The common good, however, is complex. Societies, like individuals, have a variety not just of desires, but of genuine needs. By distinguishing here between desires and needs I am trying to signal the important difference between what a particular society may have learned to value, rightly or wrongly, and what that society truly needs. Following David Wiggins, I would define a need such, that failure to satisfy a need will result in damage.

First, then, let me illustrate the difference between what is desired and what is needed. Large sections of Nazi Germany learned to desire the removal of the Jews from any active role in the community; but so far from the satisfaction of this desire being of benefit to the community as a whole, it resulted in serious damage to the common good. In fact what the community needed was the opposite of what they had learnt to desire. In practice, though, communities desire many different things – education, security, public health, a decent standard of living, employment prospects and so on. It is pretty well inevitably the case that these desires will conflict; nor is it, at least in my view, usually true to say that there is one and only one way of compromising between them which will actually work for the good of any given community at any given time. There may be several viable packages, each of which might reasonably be held to embody a version of the common good. Even if there is no one such package which is essential, the community needs one or other of them, in that if none of them were available it would suffer damage. In so far as these packages will differ to some extent in their priorities, the detailed provisions which they might make for open government may well likewise differ, and differ legitimately.

Still I take it that the avoidance of corruption and incompetence in the government of the community will be an important element in what the community needs, and hence in any viable package of goods, even though it will certainly not be the only element and there might properly be legitimate difference of opinion about how important it is. But the general question arises, is there any other good which, in particular circumstances, might conflict with the value of disclosure on demand, and which would be thought at least often to be of overriding importance? Historically it has consistently been held that there is at any rate one such value, and that is the security of the society itself. The argument is, I think, reasonable but dangerous in that it can be misused, and all too often plausibly misused.

First, it is a reasonable argument. Every citizen, and the community as a whole, has a strong interest in the stability of their society, and in preserving it from invasion, or economic collapse, or civil war. Notice, I am not saying that this is absolutely always true, nor that even when it is true the interest in social stability is an overriding one. It is not part of my argument to suggest that all revolutions are wrong, or that other forms of social instability short of revolution might not be a good thing. In extreme circumstances even these dreadful states of affairs might be the only way to achieve the long-term good of the community. Still, I assume that such circumstances will in the very nature of the case be exceptional.

Normally, stability and security are essential to the very identity of the community whose good one seeks to further. In the short term, and for that very reason, stability and security will usually override other goods which, other things being equal, one would wish to pursue. Among these goods might be competence and incorruptibility in government.

Consider this example. Let us suppose, hypothetically, that the state of Britain in 1938–39 and its unpreparedness to resist invasion was the result of incompetence in government; and suppose further that there were considerable numbers of people who would have welcomed an anti-Semitic Fascist takeover. And let us assume, less hypothetically, that a successful Nazi conquest would not have furthered the common good of British society, nor of Europe as a whole. In those circumstances, to insist on revealing the degree of governmental incompetence and the resulting military and economic weakness, and to insist on disclosing the extent of a corrupt collaborationist group might well have been disastrous. There is therefore a good argument to suggest that such considerations must take precedence over the open government which is, other things being equal, so desirable a feature of any society.

But the argument can, and often has, been misused, by representing as threats to national security disclosures which would in fact pose no threat to anyone other than the incompetent, the corrupt, or the potentially embarrassed. It is difficult to see, for example, that the revelations in *Spycatcher* really did threaten national security, and still less that this threat would have been increased if the details, already published in other countries, were to be published in Britain. Or take the case of the six Jesuit university teachers in Salvador, who were massacred by government troops for teaching social justice in their university courses. The cook, the sole survivor of the household in which they along with two of their servants were shot was subsequently hounded and considered herself under physical threat from the CIA. The CIA suspected, and with reason, that if she were allowed to give her evidence, she would reveal the extent to which they were supporting the right-wing regime in El Salvador. This revelation would have been politically highly embarrassing both to the CIA and to the Reagan administration. The details of this case are still being hushed up. Other cases, involving the granting of export licences to firms exporting to countries in the Middle East, readily come to mind.

These instances serve to make a further and most important point, to which I have already alluded. The common good requires that there should be mechanisms in place to enforce disclosure precisely in those situations in which disclosure is likely to prove embarrassing or in some other way threatening to those in power. It follows, I believe, that for the common good it must be possible for those in power to be compelled to disclose information – whether by some kind of Ombudsman, or by the Courts, or by some other traditional means. The method and the mechanism are relatively unimportant provided only that such cases, and in particular borderline cases, are not decided by those whose interests might be damaged by disclosure. Neither must they be settled by those who are all too easily convinced that the Government must have its reasons. A judge in the Clive Ponting case in effect urged the jury to agree that the government was the best judge of what was and was not a threat to national security. The jury, in my view fortunately, ignored his direction. But not all cases are simple, and disclosure is not always a good thing. We have recently seen the consequences of people believing, sometimes correctly, but in several cases mistakenly, that they had identified a paedophile living in their neighbourhood. The authors of the Johannesburg Principles themselves argue in favour of the total confidentiality of journalistic sources. All in all, I think that the conclusion must be that the onus of proof surely lies with those who seek to maintain that there are over-riding arguments in favour of secrecy; the presumption – albeit a defensible presumption – must be in favour of disclosure. The appropriate mechanisms by which the conflict between values is to be resolved must embody an attitude which I think might appropriately be described as a hermeneutic of suspicion.

The Common Good and Christian Ethics

There are doubtless also other restrictions on disclosure which can be defended, on which other speakers in this series with more legal and governmental expertise than I will surely have had much to say. But what will not have escaped your attention is the comparative lack of specifically theological argument to support the opinions which I have just expressed. I shall conclude by attempting to explain why I think this is so, and rightly so.

I have already remarked that it is, of course, not hard to find in the various theologies expressed in the biblical literature a frequently recurring emphasis on the justice of God, and God's willingness to vindicate the oppressed against their persecutors. This will readily provide a justification both for taking morality seriously, and for being especially concerned to defend the powerless against those who misuse their power. The concern in Matthew 25 for the 'least of the brethren' is surely clear enough. Moreover, it harmonizes pretty well with, for instance, John Rawls's contemporary theory of justice, in which differential treatment of people has to be justified by showing that giving preferential treatment to some is required in order to benefit the worst off. On the other hand one of my Jesuit colleagues, Garth Hallett has pointed out that whereas in Rawls there is a tendency to emphasize equality to some extent at the expense of fraternity, the emphasis for the Christian might be the other way round; we might be glad at the advantages enjoyed by others provided that these advantages are not gained at the expense of the genuine needs of others.[4] For this reason, general support in biblical and later Christian tradition for the importance of social justice is just that: it is support *in general*. Christians have found it perfectly possible to acquiesce in a wide variety of views about what is and is not in accord with justice and the common good; and certainly have not been altogether exempt from the temptation to think that any radical departure from the currently accepted view must surely be a change for the worse. While it is easy enough to point out the mistakes of past generations – their tolerance of slavery, their slowness to recognize the legitimacy of forms of government other than monarchy, and so on, it is perhaps also important to learn that justice is at the very least a many-splendoured thing; and perhaps that there is no *one* set of defensible principles of justice for all times and places, other than the most general platitudes.

We should therefore not expect to find in our tradition unambiguous guidance concerning questions about the technicalities of open government. We can, of course, say that we need whatever provisions about openness which are required to enable us to bring to account any government which, through incompetence or corruption, has turned its back on the common good and on the needs of the powerless. But *which* provisions might be needed in a given historical period, or cultural setting, or legal framework, is a complex question which can be answered only in the light of detailed legal and technical knowledge. And in matters as complex as this, the details are precisely what matters: detailed provisions, and a truly independent enforcement mechanism, both adapted to particular social and political systems. It is therefore quite unreasonable to expect to find such provisions in specifically Christian doctrine. What we can expect to find is every encouragement to look for such principles, and a general specification of the purposes which such principles should serve. They should effectively protect the weak against the abuse of power, whether the abuse is the result of incompetence, corruption, or sheer self-seeking disguised as a concern for social stability and the national interest. Christ did not teach democracy any more than he taught monarchy or oligarchy or the primacy of any political system; nor did he have a theory of human rights, any more than Aristotle or Plato did. His concerns were with fostering a society in which we care for everyone – even the least 'considerable' – as our Father in Heaven does, who numbers the hairs on each of our heads. It is up to us with our God-given minds to try to work out views of open government each of which, in its time and place, will further those concerns.

The Media We Deserve

DOUGLAS HURD

Time for Communication

The ancient Greek dramatists and philosophers tried to map out the world in which we live by the use of contrasts. One of the most frequent was the contrast between theoretical speech and practical work. 'In words on the one hand . . . in practice on the other hand . . .' provided the balance for many a sentence.

The Greeks by no means dismissed the importance of communication. Indeed it was in ancient Athens that rhetoric first assumed, at least in the Western world, the dimension of an art. But they would be amazed at the modern balance between executive action and communication. I suggest that the proportionate importance of communication as compared to decision and execution has greatly increased in the last half century, and also that this growing disproportion in favour of communication is having a powerful effect upon the decisions we take and the way our country is run.

Douglas Hurd

I have to tackle this from the experience of a politician. Let me take a trifling example. When I was Home Secretary in the late 1980s I discovered that my Private Secretaries were catching their trains home about one hour later on average than had their predecessors working for Willie Whitelaw in the same job six or seven years before. I asked them to find out why. They reported a few weeks later that the volume of advice and decision had not greatly changed. What was creating the extra hour of work was the greatly increased quantity of communication – newspaper articles, radio and television broadcasts, and consultation with outside groups. Now this was certainly not because Willie Whitelaw had been a less communicative Home Secretary; he was one of the most open in history. Over a relatively short time the *nature* of the job had shifted quite substantially, and I do not doubt that this shift has continued up to today.

Let us look at another example. When I entered the Foreign Service as a young diplomat in 1952 the Foreign Secretary was Anthony Eden, then at the height of his powers. Consider for a moment what were his duties of communication. He had of course to be attentive to the House of Commons. I suppose that he met the editor of two or three newspapers several times a year and he would broadcast occasionally on the wireless, at a time of his choosing. In these interviews he would be treated, not necessarily deferentially, but as somebody who knew his job and was likely to know more on any given foreign subject than the unqualified and unelected interviewer. That scene is totally transformed today. The Foreign

Secretary or one of his Ministers is now expected to comment within hours on any event overseas remotely affecting Britain. The interviewer is still unqualified and unelected, but is now on a level with the Minister, or indeed the Vice Chancellor of a University or the Chairman of a company. If within say twenty four hours of a dramatic overseas event the Foreign Secretary cannot declare a Government attitude or policy then clearly, it is supposed, the man is losing his grip. But within that period of time it is often completely impossible to have any kind of balanced, accurate account of what has occurred. Ted Heath, when I worked for him, taught me one lesson which I found particularly useful as Home Secretary: the first account which you receive of any sudden event will be wrong.

In Anthony Eden's time Britain fought a war in Oman on behalf of our friend and ally the Sultan against some of his rebel subjects up in the mountains. This war dragged on and eventually succeeded, but was almost entirely secret until after it was won. Compare what happened recently when British soldiers were kidnapped by rebels in Sierra Leone. The whole danger and embarrassment had to be worked through in a full blaze of publicity, with Ministers being summoned on to radio and television several times a day.

Whenever one begins to develop this line of argument, journalists are quick to suppose that we politicians are yearning nostalgically for the censor's pen. That would be quite unrealistic. They are right about this. I believe that where there is blood on the streets there ought to be

Douglas Hurd

blood on the television screen. I am certainly not in favour, even if it were feasible, of British Governments concealing facts from the public. In our time together in Government, William Waldegrave and I opened a good many secret cupboards. But there is a twist in the argument here of which I do not believe the public is always aware. The phrase 'freedom of information' comprises two different concepts. The first is the individual citizen having direct access to information affecting his life, for example his health, or the risks of a particular development or policy or discovery which affects him. Separate from this is the concept that the journalist should have access *on behalf of the citizen* to almost all matters of public concern. The first, or direct freedom of information, is an undoubted good. The worth of the second, or indirect freedom, depends on the worth of the media through which the information passes.

The Media as a Lens

At present, and I underline at present, citizens rely almost totally on the media for our perception of public affairs, and the quantity of media available to meet our requirements has exploded. In this context freedom of information means freedom for the media, with the citizen (it is hoped) benefiting at one remove.

All the more important that we should understand the nature of the lens which the media provide for us. It distorts. When I use the word distort I am not bringing a criminal charge, but describing an optical condition, or rather a series of optical conditions. As the mass of information pouring in upon us hour by hour from all continents of the world increases, it is the more important if we are to evaluate it sensibly that we understand the nature of the glass through which we are viewing.

These distortions are several. The easiest to identify are of course those of opinion. The leader writer, the newspaper columnist or the television commentator states a point of view, namely his own, and analyses the facts against that viewpoint. No-one could possibly object to that in a society where the citizen has choice. The distinction drawn by the old *Manchester Guardian* was crisp: comment is free, facts are sacred. You will know of the cynical adaptation in more recent times: comment is free, facts are expensive. Whether for this reason or another, a modern British broadsheet newspaper contains a much higher proportion of comment to fact than its predecessor did half a century ago. Moreover the selection and presentation of facts will depend to a substantial extent on the general policy of the newspaper. The account of events in Germany in any given year appearing in a British newspaper will depend on the general view of that newspaper towards the European Union, the *euro*, Germany and so on. You will not find eurosceptic newspapers detaining their readers for long on the superiority of French productivity over our own, or the glittering French trading performance. Nor will you find in the *New York Times* or other East Coast American papers as sympathetic an account of the

Palestinian plight on the West Bank as you would find in most British and other European papers.

Other distortions are less obvious and therefore more damaging. The commercial pressures on a newspaper drive it towards the dramatic, and this is also true of radio and television. This amounts to saying that readers and viewers like to have it both ways. We like to be educated, but we also like to be excited and entertained. That is why the broadsheets drift downwards towards the tabloids. Indeed the honest desire of the tabloid to entertain, because it is so clear, is perhaps less of a distortion than some developments of the broadsheet, for example the acres of gossip which pass for parliamentary reporting in this country.

This appetite for excitement produces odd results in the field of risk. Much of today's reporting is in one way or another concerned with risk. We have recently had a notable example. A rail crash is a dramatic, highly visual tragedy which fortunately occurs fairly rarely, and certainly less often in this country than it did at the beginning of the last century. Rail travel is much safer than air travel or road travel. Yet a multiple road crash in which say four people were killed might attract momentary attention in a few bulletins on one day, compared with the domination of the headlines day after day by the Hatfield rail disaster. There are various defensible reasons for this. For example a rail crash is likely to involve more matters of public policy than a road crash. For that reason it looks and sounds more political, or at least a strong effort is mounted to make it so. Nevertheless we should be aware of the distortion and perhaps ask whether £x million spent on safer roads would save more lives than the same sum spent by Railtrack on safer rail. Alongside the zest for drama comes the tendency to personalize, to insist on both heroes and villains. This particularly comes to the fore after an accident, or a particularly wicked crime. Victims are pitchforked into a certain position. At the time of their deepest unhappiness victims are tempted and expected to pick up the role not just of grieving relative or friend, but of technical expert, judge and jury. The parents of the victims of the Dunblane shooting, the parents of James Bulger, the parents more recently of Sarah Payne, the relatives of BSE sufferers – we can all remember how the modern media half tempted, half propelled these individuals into the limelight.

I have moved rapidly, and therefore superficially, over some of the differences which I have seen media perception make to the decisions taken by governments on our behalf. It is worth repeating in the light of Lord Philips' report on BSE that what Ministers and Civil Servants have to cope with in handling questions of public risk is not just how the citizen will react, but how he or she will react after the media have conveyed the data through the particular lenses of their trade.

The Media at War

Similar pressures are exerted in reporting dramatic events on the battlefield. Max Hastings is one of the most expert, and perhaps the wisest of our foreign correspondents. It is worth quoting two sentences from his recent book *Going to the Wars*:

> The overwhelming majority of alleged combat sequences shot on film in the twentieth century and screened and transmitted again and again as authentic are in reality, fakes – or at least heavily embellish the nature of the experience they purport to show. Every knowledgeable and honest television documentary-maker knows this.[1]

I do not think I need elaborate. The camera is an actor. Its presence on the scene influences, say, the youths throwing stones or the sniper at the window. But this leads to a wider point. The striking new *public* dimension of international diplomatic and military action has implications which go well beyond anything I can describe adequately here. After the Suez campaign of 1956 there were many post mortems. Perhaps the conclusion most often drawn in this country was the one on which Harold Macmillan acted throughout his premiership, namely that we must never again get involved in an enterprise of comparable substance without American support. The Commander of the Allied Force which invaded Egypt, General Keighley, drew another more far reaching conclusion: 'The overriding lesson of the Suez operation is that world opinion is now an absolute principle of war and must be treated as such.' The British General in 1957 intended a negative, namely that you could not invade another country against the force of world public opinion as portrayed through the media. In 1999 the British Prime Minister in Chicago turned that round to a positive proposition and described the circumstances in which public opinion, again expressed through the media, would induce Britain to intervene with a military force in somebody else's civil war in order to stop barbarities.

Tony Blair was making a British contribution to the evolution of the doctrine of humanitarian war. The debate is still at a fairly early stage and no satisfactory answer has yet been found to the two main drawbacks of the new doctrine. First, its application can run counter to international law. International law requires the Security Council to authorize intervention in such cases, and this did not happen in Kosovo. Second, humanitarian intervention will be partially not universally practised. We shall pick and choose. In practice international intervention will only take place against those who are not closely linked to the great powers, and who cannot effectively resist them. This is not an argument against the new doctrine of humanitarian intervention; it is three years since I wrote, 'We are all interventionists now.' But it is an argument against standing on a pulpit to proclaim it as if it had some universal ethical content.

It is worth noting that in such cases the material passes twice through the lens of the media. First the facts on the ground are reported to the citizens, and here we remember Max Hastings' caveat. Second the reaction of the citizen, for example the feeling that 'something must be done' reaches the politician very largely through the media, for example in opinion polls or leading articles.

Living with Lenses

Before you conclude that I am hopelessly obscurantist I repeat that I do not believe that government can or should attempt to clear these different distortions from the lenses through which the media invite us to enjoy freedom of information. For two years I lived in the People's Republic of China just after the Communist Revolution of 1949. No-one who has worked in a total-itarian country can feel anything but revulsion at the way in which the citizen is patronized and pap-fed with information. The distortions of that approach are infin-itely greater than those which I have been describing. It does not follow, however, that we can be satisfied with what we have. On the contrary I believe that we should be much more critical of the critics. We are developing in Britain a bias, not against this party or that party, but against people who run things. Too much of our talent goes into criticism of one kind or another.

Criticism is an essential part of a healthy society. If it becomes over-dominant then the performance of that society dwindles as talent ebbs out of achievement into criticism. Anyone who runs a school or an NHS Trust or company or indeed a railway line knows that there is truth in this worry.

It is possible that the problem which I have been analysing will soon change quite dramatically. We are not yet clear about the effect of the Internet upon these arguments. The pessimist sees fraud and corruption on the web. The optimist says that the Internet will give the individual citizen access to truth *without a lens*, to a whole mass of actual facts and documents that will not have to be summarized, selected, annotated by a newspaper or television company. On subjects of our choice we will be able to range absolutely freely and fully. Real freedom of information means freedom from the media as well as from government.

Is that at last going to be attainable? The difficulty lies with ourselves. Technology has transformed most aspects of communication, but not ourselves. The poor antiquated human being still has only twenty four hours in a day and seven days in a week, and needs to sleep during some of them. Someone else will have to lecture you on the genetic changes needed to remedy this weakness. Meanwhile we must learn to use criticism to achieve reform, without allowing it to swamp our lives and turn us into cynics; and try to multiply the occasions when, even in this world, we can see, not through a glass darkly, but face to face.

Afterword

JOHN MAJOR

'Believe, believe – I've never believed in anything in my life!' So retorted Sir Humphrey Appleby in one episode of that memorable satire of parliamentary life *Yes, Prime Minister*. Sir Humphrey's overreaction was in response to one of his colleagues who had begun, 'But surely Sir Humphrey you believe in . . .' To the outsider, belief or more accurately conviction is the last virtue to be assigned to the professional politician. Indeed politics itself is seen to smack of manipulation, duplicity and an overdose of guile. Regrettably this cynical perception has increased rather than decreased in many Western democracies. The critical tools that abound, not least in the press and media, mean that nothing is sacred or beyond reproof. Paradoxically our ability to apply a critical eye to our institutions has not strengthened those institutions by opening them to sharp scrutiny. Instead it has increased public cynicism at what is believed to be the corruption of, or at the very least obscuring of, accountability within government. This suspicion and uncertainty takes us to the heart of the issues explored by the contributions in this book. For not only must 'justice be done, it must be seen to be done'. The same is true of government; not only should it be good but it should be accountable and open to scrutiny.

As someone who has experienced it for more than half a lifetime, nothing can be more exhilarating than political life. All the way from telling outside polling stations, to awaiting with bated breath the pronouncements of the returning officer, or to embarking for the first time on ministerial office and receiving one's first despatch boxes - involvement in politics and in government helps to keep the levels of adrenalin high. Part of this is the result of wishing to play a part in fashioning the future of one's world, to be part of the decision-making process which will improve quality of life, and to be offering oneself for public service. All this runs in almost direct contrast to the avowed cynicism of Sir Humphrey's denial of any real commitment or belief. But to achieve these high aims is very different from simply avowing them as one's interest. How is one to undermine the electorate's cynicism about politicians?

This question stood at the heart of my aim in the early 1990s to make government and our public institutions more accountable. The Citizens' Charter, which did not always enjoy a good press, stood central to these aims. My desire was for nothing less than an information revolution. Therein lies the basis for declaring standards for every public service. It has to be said that, predictably, institutions were rarely enthusiastic about moving down this particular road. There was a widespread reluctance to publish information or to open one's organization to independent inspection. Admittedly we did not always get it right. Individuals and institutions are easily threatened and on occasion we may have taken too little care to see how best to handle such insecurity. Nevertheless in retrospect I remain unrepentant about moving along this road. The essays in this book seem to me to reinforce the appropriateness of this attempted shift towards a greater openness.

In his penetrating and swashbuckling contribution, Peter Hennessy paints a vivid picture, as is always the case in his political commentary; he indicates just how far we have moved toward more open government. That splendid quotation from the *Questions of Procedure*, dating from the time of Lord Attlee's government, and then that marvellous brief from Sir William Armstrong indicate the progress that has been made since those days. Armstrong's wording indicates fairly clearly why cynicism may build up within the electorate. It includes a paternalistic assumption that the general public should only be given the information that politicians and Whitehall mandarins believe would be good for them. My desire to work for greater openness, however, both here and more widely with the Citizens' Charter, goes deeper than this. One of my abiding aversions as a politician has been to any form of ideology. This aversion seems to me to run deep in the British bloodstream and, at its best, the Conservative party has represented a tradition in British politics which has stood clear of ideological obsessions. In his introduction to these essays, the Dean of Norwich begins with that whimsical reference to the stolen Kremlin election results. One of the depressing features of most totalitarian regimes, and particularly of governments during the Soviet period in Russia and Eastern Europe, was an obsessive control of information which was itself a direct function of ideological trends. This is why I believe the sort of openness for which I continue to strive lies at the heart of true democracy.

I was also interested to read in the essays references to changes in reporting and the way the press and media cover politics and public life. Douglas Hurd, my former colleague, makes this clear most elegantly in his contribution. Furthermore, almost as an aside he also makes it clear that although open reporting and critical journalism are crucial, balance and care are still essential. Ironically an over-developed critical society can evade the very openness which such criticism sets out to provide. Institutions need to be accountable but they also need to be nourished. The undermining of organizations as a result of sniping and snide criticism will not be nourishing to democracy. Consistently rapacious reporting of the Royal Family, of the Church and of other national institutions is threatening to weaken the fibre of our national life. There is bound, then, to be a tension between providing an appropriate and real accountability by means of effective journalism and a less positive tendency towards deliberately subversive reporting. Kate Adie has effectively made her name by riding the storm caused by such a tension. In her essay that process is well demonstrated. She makes it clear that it is, on occasion, what the public will support and find acceptable that limits the freedom of journalists. She quotes the frequently used adage 'knowledge is power'. To keep people in ignorance is not to serve the public interest. That is precisely what stands behind my commitment to a greater openness in government and in our national institutions. We cannot expect our society to act responsibly if we starve them of knowledge and assume that no further material should be made available since society is insufficiently mature to know how best to handle that newly released information.

Part of the duty of a government is to nourish the reciprocal responsibilities of the electorate and the political administration. A democratic society rests upon a mutual trust between those who for a five-year term have been given the responsibility to govern and the society which is being governed. Increased cynicism is partly the result of a starvation of knowledge or information; this all too often stems from an insecurity within those institutions who act as guardians of that knowledge, and this often means government departments. Paternalism can easily fuel an increased sense of stratification and hence ossification in society. From taking up my responsibilities as Prime Minister I was keen to avoid this and to work for 'classlessness' in British society. Part of such a classless Britain must issue from government and other institutions and organizations trusting people from different backgrounds and contexts with as much access to information as is effectively possible.

In his closely argued philosophical analysis of open

government, Gerard Hughes roots much of his support
for the concept in the ideas of 'common good'. This idea,
I realise, finds its origins in theological reflection upon
which I would not feel qualified to comment. Nevertheless, the images that Father Hughes brings to bear offer
models that are resonant with those which underpin
democratic government in a consultative society. It is as
important for politicians as it is for theologians to stress
the significance of the human family. I also have sympathy
with his uncertainty about applying the language of
rights in every aspect of human endeavour and association. This was one of the reasons why the government
which I led had reservations about the European Social
Charter. Father Hughes' philosophical reservations here
may support some of the more pragmatic and practical
reasons as to why rights language is sometimes less
popular with politicians than might be expected in a
democratic society. Fundamental human rights are
essential to supporting a civilized society, but as rights
proliferate they can bear less political weight.

Another 'theological' point attracted my interest
towards the end of the introduction. Stephen Platten
refers there to the consultative model embraced by the
abbot in St Benedict's monastic communities. This
kindled a thought in relation to the development of
democracy in this country. Britain, or at least England,
has been justly proud of her tradition of parliamentary
government reaching back at least in an embryonic form
to the thirteenth century. As that model evolved, so a
relatively compact group of ministers took responsibility

for advising the sovereign and then later the Prime Minister. The Privy Council was just one such body; it was an inner group charged with steering some of the highest matters of state. In the twentieth century cabinet government was based on a similar principle. It is interesting to speculate as to whether St Benedict's abbot consulting with his monks might have been one of the seeds for the development of cabinet corporate responsibility. If this is the case, then we have much to thank St Benedict for; corporate responsibility is essential to good government. In his remarkable history of the office of Prime Minister, both in terms of function and personalities, Peter Hennessy makes much of the key role that cabinet government and responsibility has had within British democracy.[1] Indeed in reviewing each Prime Minister since 1945 that is one of the key elements of his analysis. As he indicates, the fortunes of true cabinet responsibility ebb and flow: but it is my view that the present government, as led by the Prime Minister, is doing serious damage to this vital component in the governance of the United Kingdom. Nevertheless it would be churlish to argue that this is cabinet government's first fall from grace; both Labour and Conservative Prime Ministers have used this instrument to greater and lesser degrees. I have been criticized on occasion for an over-consultative style. It is a criticism for which I do not repent. My guess is that St Benedict got it right when he aimed to focus consensus through a consultative model of leadership. That seems to me to be a seminal element within the development of open government.

Afterword

In the final chapter of my autobiography I wrote: 'We must now improve the openness and accountability of the government to parliament and people . . . The accountability of the government will improve by making parliament more efficient and more effective. A toothless parliament goes with unaccountable government. Only a government with teeth can yield genuine accountability.'[2] I am clear that such principles can only be achieved if 'government is not only done but is seen to be done'. At the heart of such principles lie both freedom of information and open government. The more that we can move genuinely in that direction rooting the leadership of our nation in a truly consultative parliamentary system based on effective cabinet government, the more we shall undermine the understandable cynicism of the electorate. This means the avoidance of presidential government and the sidelining of parliament, an ever present danger even in British-style democracies and another source of electoral cynicism. It is such cynicism which breeds apathy and a lack of desire to engage with the electoral process. For all these reasons I welcome these contributions and the imaginative ways in which the authors have tackled issues which are crucial to the health of British democracy and indeed democracy in the free world.

Notes

Introduction: Stephen Platten

1. House of Commons, Select Committee on Public Administration, Session 1998–99, Third Report, *Freedom of Information Draft Bill*, Vol. I, HMSO, July 1999.
2. See p. 37.
3. John Hands, *Perestroika Christi*, Simon & Schuster, London, 1990.
4. Ibid., p. 113.
5. *The Common Good, A statement by the Catholic Bishops' Conference of England and Wales*, Gabriel Publications, Manchester, 1996, p. 5.
6. Karl Popper, *The Open Society and Its Enemies*, Vols I & II, 1944, 2nd edn, 1950.
7. John Habgood, 'Public Life and Private Life' in *Church and Nation in a Secular Age*, Darton, Longman and Todd, London, 1983, p. 54
8. Reinhold Niebuhr, *Moral Man and Immoral Society*, Charles Scribners, New York, 1932.
9. Reinhold Niebuhr, *The Irony of American History*, Nisbet, London, 1952, p. 54.

2. 'The Long March?': Peter Hennessy

1. 'City Notes, The Fate of Steel', *The Times*, 25 March 1946.

Notes

2. Ibid.
3. Public Record Office, PREM 8/156, 'Future of the Steel Industry: Leakage of Information,' Brook to Attlee, 3 April 1946.
4. Quoted in Peter Hennessy, *What the Papers Never Said*, Politicos, 1985, p. 141.
5. PRO, PREM 8/156, Brook to Attlee, 3 April 1946.
6. Ibid. Extract from the Cabinet Minutes for 4 April 1946 (CC (46) 30, item 2).
7. Ibid. Jowett to Attlee, 18 April 1946.
8. Ibid. 'Leakage of Information Memorandum by the Prime Minister', CP (46)163, 29 April 1946.
9. Amy Baker, *Prime Ministers and the Rule Book*, Politicos, 2000, p. xii, pp. 59–71; Peter Hennessy, *The Prime Minister: The Office and its Holders since 1945*, Penguin, 2000, p. 451.
10. PRO, CAB 129/ CP (49)95, 'Questions of Procedure for Ministers', 29 April 1949.
11. PRO, CAB 129/1966.
12. PRO, CAB 171/9, 'Questions of Procedure for Ministers', C (PR) (76) 1, 23 April 1976.
13. *Cabinet Committee Business: A Guide for Departments*, Cabinet Office, January 2000.
14. Bruce Page, 'The Secret Constitution', *New Statesman*, 21 July 1976; Peter Hennessy, *Cabinet*, Blackwell, 1986, pp. 27–30.
15. James Margach, *The Abuse of Power: The War Between Downing Street and the Media from Lloyd George to James Callaghan*, W. H. Allen, London, 1978, p. 1.
16. For the early history of the Westminster Lobby see James Margach, *The Anatomy of Power – An Enquiry into the Personality of Leadership*, W. H. Allen, London, 1979, Chapter 9, 'The Lobby', pp. 125–56.
17. Francis Willams, *Parliament, Press and the Public*, Heinemann, London, 1946, pp. 136–7.

Notes

18. PRO, PREM 11/732, 'Arrangements for briefing the Lobby: Lord Swinton and the Chancellor of the Exchequer proposed as spokesmen', Fife Clark to Churchill.
19. Ibid.
20. *The Civil Service, Vol. 1, Report of the Committee 1966–68*, Cmnd 3638, HMSO, London, 1968, pp. 104–6.
21. *Information and the Public Interest*, Cmnd 4089, HMSO, London, 1969, p. 11.
22. Ibid.
23. *Departmental Committee on Section 2 of the Official Secrets Act 1911, Vol. 1, Report of the Committee*, Cmnd 5104, HMSO, London, 1972.
24. David Vincent, *The Culture of Secrecy: Britain 1832–1998*, Oxford University Press, Oxford, 1998, p. 307.
25. PRO, PREM 13/2528, 'Fulton Report: Government's consideration of recommendations: Enquiry into release of official information and Official Secrets Act, Part 2'.
26. See Ronald Robinson and John Gallagher with Alice Denny, *Africa and the Victorians: The Official Mind of Imperialism*, Macmillan, London, 1965.
27. See, for example, PRO, PREM 13/1798, 'Procedures for handling Cabinet and Cabinet committee papers in departments: need to avoid the risk of leaks.'
28. PRO, PREM 13/1077, 'Personal Minutes from Prime Minister to Ministers 1966', Wilson to Crossman, 22 December 1966.
29. PRO, PREM 13/2528, Halls to Walker, 23 January 1969.
30. 'Heath pleads for Official Secrets Act review,' *Daily Telegraph*, 8 January 1969.
31. The speech was delivered on 23 January 1969. Its text is preserved in PRO, PREM 13/2528.
32. Ibid. Shackleton to Wilson, 23 February 1969.
33. Ibid. Halls to Wilson, 21 February 1969.
34. Ibid. 'The Release of Official Information.' Brief for the Prime Minister and the Lord Privy Seal, 5 March 1969.

Notes

35. Ibid.
36. Ibid.
37. Ibid.
38. James Cameron, *Cameron in The Guardian 1974–1984*, Hutchinson, London, 1985, p. 85. This delicious phrase first appeared in 'Plumb Censorship' published by *The Guardian* on 20 December 1983.
39. Ibid.
40. (On 21 March 1969.) Ibid. Armstrong to Halls, 22 April 1969.
41. House of Commons, Select Committee on Public Administration, Session 1998–99, Third Report, *Freedom of Information Draft Bill*, Vol. 1, HMSO, London, July 1999.
42. Private information.
43. *Code of Practice on Access to Government Information*, Cabinet Office/OPSS, 1994.
44. Peter Hennessy, *The Prime Minister: The Office and its Holders since 1945*, Penguin, London, 2000, p. 452; David Wilkinson, 'Open Government: The Development of Policy in the United Kingdom in the 1990s' in Andrew McDonald and Greg Terrill (eds.), *Open Government: Freedom of Information and Privacy*, Macmillan, London, 1998, pp. 13–24.
45. Letter from Dr Andrew McDonald, Head of the Records Management Department of the Public Record Office to Peter Hennessy, 22 November 1999; Andrew McDonald, 'Archives and Open Government', in McDonald and Terrill (eds.) *Open Government*, pp. 25–44.
46 Conversation with Sir John Browne, 15 November 1999.
47. Sir John Hoskyns, The Institute of Directors Lecture, 28 September 1983.
48. *The BSE Inquiry, Vol 1: Findings and Conclusions*, House of Commons 887–1, HMSO, London, 2000, pp. 264–6.

49. 'Heath pleads for Official Secrets Act review'.
50. Quoted in Michael Cockerell, Peter Hennessy and David Walker, *Sources Close to the Prime Minister: Inside the hidden world of the news manipulators*, Macmillan, London, 1984, p. 89.

3. *God, Morals and Secrecy: Gerard J. Hughes*

1. In Sandra Coliver (ed.), *Secrecy and Liberty*, Martinus Nijhoff, The Hague & London, 1999.
2. Geoffrey Chapman, *Catechism of the Catholic Church*, London, 1994, paragraph 2483.
3. James Madison, letter of 1822.
4. Garth Hallett SJ, *Christian Moral Reasoning*, Notre Dame Press, 1983, pp 154–55.

4. *The Media We Deserve: Douglas Hurd*

1. Max Hastings, *Going to the Wars*, Macmillan, London, 2000, pp. 416.

Afterword: John Major

1. Peter Hennessy, *The Prime Minister: The Office and Its Holders Since 1945*, Allen Lane, The Penguin Press, London, 2001.
2. John Major, *The Autobiography*, HarperCollins, London, 1999, p. 747.